CONTENTS

ABOUT THE AUTHOR

This book combines two of Deanna Hall West's greatest loves—beautiful hand-crafted needlework and nature's amazing flowers.

Her professional positions in the needlework field have included Features Editor for two national needlework magazines. She is currently the Creative Director for Kooler Design Studio in Pleasant Hill, California. This creative group designs much of the excellent cross stitch published by the American School of Needlework®.

Deanna's experience in the world of flowers includes both bachelor's and master's degrees in botany and work as research associate in botany at University of California, Berkeley.

She describes her childhood in Missoula, Montana as idyllic, and plans to go back to Montana someday for a dinosaur dig.

INTRODUCTION

Ribbon embroidery is fun, easy, and exciting! The three-dimensional effect of this soft, tactile form of needlework is one of its most endearing qualities. Ribbon embroidery does use a few unique stitching techniques, but they are simple and easily learned.

Today there is a new appreciation and heightened interest in the old needleart form of ribbon embroidery. Both silk ribbon and the new synthetic ribbons (with similar properties and the feel of silk, but less fragile) are now more readily available than ever before. This coincides with the many new how-to and design books now being marketed in the United States and abroad (particularly Australia, New Zealand, and South Africa).

Ribbon embroidery first became popular during the French Rococo period (1750-1780s) when the attire of royalty and the court ladies was profusely decorated with sprays of ribbonwork done by the professional stitchers from "officially sanctioned" embroidery houses. The privilege of wearing these elaborately embroidered gowns was reserved solely for the French royalty and its court. However, not to be outdone, the British court soon adopted this extravagant fashion of rosettes, ruching, and ribbonwork.

At various intervals since the 18th century, embroidery with ribbon has enjoyed off-and-on interest. From the 1820s until World War I ribbon embroidery appeared on men's waistcoats, sewing accessories, samplers, Baltimore Album and crazy quilts, clothing, hats, purses, and in home decor.

In the 1980s, ribbon embroidery slowly started to emerge from a lengthy dormant period to its present day explosion. This current wave of interest can be credited to several Australian ribbonworkers with more teachers and stitchers appearing in the United States, New Zealand, and South Africa.

There may be many ways to stitch a particular flower or plant which will give a recognizable result; however, we have chosen versions that are easily workable and also highly effective. Occasionally we show one or more examples of a flower. There is a beautiful array of 17 rose variations. On pages 21-60, directions are given for working each of the flowers shown stitched in the color photographs on pages 17-20 and the covers. We have included common and exotic garden and house plants, some foliage, plus garden critters and decorative bows.

Supplies

Ribbon

Ribbons used for embroidery are chosen for their special properties. They must drape nicely and be able to be pulled through fabric without damage to the ribbon or the fabric. Silk and the recently manufactured silk substitutes (silky polyester and rayon) can be used for embroidery.

For ribbon embroidery, 4mm is the most commonly used ribbon width, and different companies have a wide range of 4mm colors. The 2mm and 7mm ribbons are also used, although the color range is more limited. Mixing ribbon widths adds to the textural contrast which is a strong aspect of this embroidery.

Silk ribbon should be stored so that no sharp creases are formed. Some ribbon brands come with their own plastic storage reels. However, you can create your own storage rolls for ribbon. Cut a paper tube into 1" segments, cover each roll with acid-free paper and wind each ribbon color around a roll.

Work with ribbon cut into 10"-12" (or shorter) pieces. Embroidery ribbons are relatively fragile, and during the stitching process the ribbon can be easily damaged. Short lengths help to prevent damage.

The stitching directions list the colors used for the flowers shown in the color section on pages 17-20 and the back cover. Refer to the Ribbon Color Conversion Key on page 16 for suggestions when substituting different brands of ribbon. Color ranges vary greatly between companies, so you can really choose whatever colors you want based on what is readily available and your own personal preference.

Threads

Six-strand cotton embroidery floss is occasionally used with ribbon to create narrow lines of embroidery, tack down a portion of a stitch, or preserve a special shape. When floss is required for the construction of a flower, we have listed a generic color name for the floss, usually to match

the ribbon with which it is used. You can also use any of the following embroidery threads with great success:

Crewel yarn, very fine wool
Floche, five-ply cotton
Flower thread, twisted matte-finish cotton
Marlitt or similar-weight rayon thread
Pearl cotton, size 8 and occasionally size 5
Silk, seven-strand floss

Needles

Basically, three types of needles are used for ribbon embroidery. We find that all kinds have their place. You can choose a sharp chenille needle or a blunt tapestry needle; a crewel needle is used for fine threads.

One important factor to consider when choosing the correct needle is the size of the eye. With silk ribbon the needle's eye should be large enough for the ribbon to pass through easily, with little or no gathering. Also, the size of the needle's shaft needs to be large enough that a sufficient hole is made in the background to accommodate the ribbon as it passes through the fabric without causing too much friction, which can further damage the ribbon. In sizing, the higher the number, the smaller the needle.

(continued)

A chenille needle is a large sharp needle with a large eye. Size 18 chenille is used for most embroidery with 4mm- and 7mm-wide ribbon. Size 20 can be used with the 2mm-wide ribbon. Packages of chenille needles which include sizes 18-22 are the best assortment.

A tapestry needle, with a blunt tip, of a size equivalent to the sharp chenille needle can be used if the ribbon embroidery is to be done on linen or one of the popular evenweave fabrics. You can also use a tapestry needle any time you want to be sure not to pierce the threads of the background fabric or any of the stitching ribbon.

An embroidery or crewel needle is a fine sharp needle with a large eye. This needle style is appropriate when embellishing a ribbon design with floss, silk thread, or any of the other accessory threads. The needle size will depend on the thread size and the number of strands used. An assortment package with sizes 3 to 9 will be very useful.

Fabrics

Any fabric with a medium weave will work as a background fabric. Knitted fabrics are often too loose to hold ribbon embroidery securely, but can be used if a lightweight non-stretch backing fabric is attached.

Some fabric suggestions are:
Dressmaking fabrics—cottons, voile, silks, batiste, faille
Evenweave embroidery fabrics—plain weaves like linen, cottage cloth, Jobelan®, Lugana, or complex weaves like Aida and hardanger
Linen twill—often used for crewel embroidery
Specially-packaged ribbon embroidery fabric

For ribbon-embellished clothing, choose a fabric that does not require much ironing. A lightweight interfacing can be attached to the back of the fabric to prevent puckering around the embroidery. The garment needs to be laundered according to the ribbon manufacturer's washing instructions.

Simple stitches, such as French Knots, Lazy Daisy Stitches, Ribbon Stitches, and Straight Stitches, work best for clothing. Avoid pressing ribbon embroidery.

The back of ribbon embroidery is certainly not neat! If you are working on a ready-made garment, you might wish to remove enough of the lining to do your stitching, then replace the lining to cover the back of your work. If there is no lining, consider attaching a soft material to the wrong side of the stitching area.

Frames and Hoops

The best ribbon embroidery results are achieved when the background fabric is held under tension during the stitching process. Use an appropriately sized embroidery hoop, especially when working on clothing, or needlework stretcher bars. If the previously worked stitching needs to be held in place while constructing the next petals or leaves, you will need a small hoop so you can hold with one hand and stitch with the other.

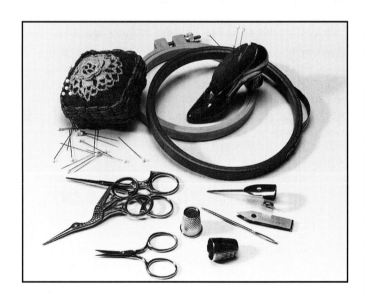

Scissors

Small, sharp embroidery scissors are needed. Besides cutting the ribbon and embroidery threads, the flat surface of the blade, used in a stroking manner, can help to spread the ribbon where it emerges from the fabric.

Additional Handy Tools

The following inexpensive needlework tools or accessories are helpful in creating a beautifully finished project:

Cotton swab, lightly moistened—to remove any marks on the fabric that are not covered by your embroidery

Drinking straw, knitter's cable holder, knitting needle, #13 yarn needle or pencil—to help make ribbon loops of equal length

Marking pens or pencils—to transfer a design on the background fabric, if desired; use a water-soluble fabric-marking pen or a white pencil for dark fabrics

Silk pins—to hold ribbon loops and stitches in place (ordinary sewing pins create large holes in the ribbon)

Stilletto, awl or large-diameter sharp needle—to puncture holes into tightly woven background fabric and prevent wide ribbon from being damaged

Tapestry needle (#18 or larger) or a trolley needle—to manipulate, spread, and adjust the silk ribbon

🌸 **Special Techniques**

Marking Designs on Fabric—Often, ribbon embroidery is worked with just a position mark on the fabric, rather than a full pattern. This approach works especially well for designs like the flowers shown in this book. Draw a basic stem line, then locations for the intended flowers, buds, and leaves, and stitch accordingly.

If you prefer, you may draw the outline of a design on the background. Place fabric directly over the design and trace with water-soluble fabric-marking pen or pencil. If the fabric is heavy, a lightbox will be helpful. You can also use lead pencil (for light to medium-colored fabrics) or white pencil (for dark fabrics).

Threading the Needle—Always cut your ribbon into short lengths for stitching; we recommend 10"-12". Thread the end through the eye, and pull it through beyond the tip of the needle. Pierce the ribbon end with the needle, **Fig 1**. Holding point of needle, pull the long end of the ribbon to secure it.

Fig 1

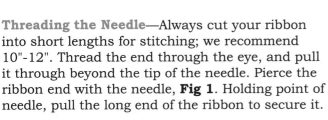

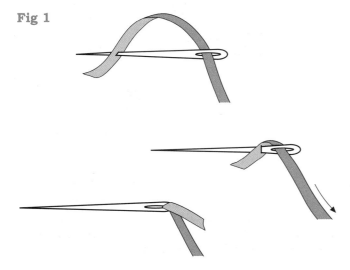

Making a Knot—To begin stitching, make this special knot, **Fig 2**, at end of ribbon. Drape ribbon end over needle; wrap working ribbon once around needle, then pull needle through the wrap to form a knot. When you begin to stitch, be careful not to pull too tightly, or the knot may come through the fabric.

Fig 2

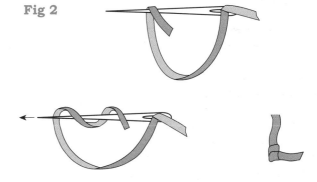

Ending the Ribbon—When you finish using a color, run the needle under a few stitches on the wrong side, **Fig 3**. The ribbon should end, whenever possible, toward the center of the stitching area to avoid being visible beyond the edge of the embroidery. If desired, pierce through some ribbon on the back before cutting the end, but make sure this does not disturb the front of your work.

Fig 3

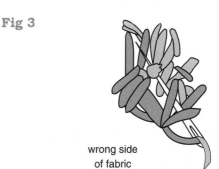

wrong side
of fabric

Stitching Tips ❀

- Use short ribbon lengths (10"-12") to prevent excessive ribbon damage.
- Lightly mark background fabric with pencil to indicate the spokes for a Spider Web or placement of petals around an open area.
- Keep a #18 tapestry needle handy for spreading and manipulating the silk ribbon into smooth, beautiful stitches.
- Keep ribbon untwisted on the back of the fabric; this makes it easier to spread out the stitches on the front of the fabric.
- Nudge the needle tip around ribbon that is on the back of the fabric as you find the correct stitching location. Avoid stitching through ribbon or knots on the back. If your stitching ribbon is pulled through an already-worked stitch, it can cause distortion or damage to the existing stitch.
- Use thumb (even thumbnail!) and forefinger of your non-stitching hand to hold previously worked stitches in place while working the next adjacent stitch. This helps prevent previous stitches from being pulled too tightly or even being rearranged into visual disarray.
- You may be working with two threaded needles (perhaps one with silk ribbon and the other with floss) at the same time. To prevent a tangled mess and pulled stitches, bring the needle temporarily to rest on the front of the fabric, parking it away from the working area. You can also hold excess ribbon out of the way with a long silk pin.
- The stiffer the ribbon, the larger the stitches tend to be. You can compensate for this natural trend by pulling the stitches more tightly.

Special Notes About Flowers ❀

Remember that Mother Nature is not perfect, so our ribbon flowers do not have to be perfect either. And it's okay to have partial flowers, because the local neighborhood garden critter may have had a snack!

Add side views of flowers and leaves whenever possible for a more naturalistic garden scene or floral arrangement.

Not all flowers and leaves on the same plant should be the same size. Young flowers just out of the bud stage and new leaves tend to be smaller than older flowers and leaves. You can change the scale by using different ribbon widths and by the tension of your stitching. Also, remember that there are miniature roses and giant pansies available now, so take license with the scale of the flowers and leaves.

When planning your project, use the following sources as inspiration for floral arrangements; flower color; general plant appearance; and flower, bud, and leaf structure:

Bulb and seed catalogs
Plant and garden design books and magazines
Wildflower field guides
Flower arranging books
General botany and horticulture books

Finishing ❀

If your piece was worked on a frame, there will probably be no blocking required. If the finished embroidery is to be washed, pre-test the ribbon to make sure it is colorfast. Dip a small piece in water and place on a paper towel; let dry and check to see if the dye runs. If the ribbon is not colorfast, but the item must be washed, choose another ribbon. If you must wash, use cold water with mild soap and a cold water rinse.

When working on a ready-made garment, take into account the surface fabric needs as well as the embroidery. If you must take an iron to it, press face down on a thick padded surface—a terry cotton towel is an excellent choice—only lightly pressing the areas of stitching. Use caution to prevent scorching.

When framing, you may wish to protect the embroidery with glass. Because of the textural quality, choose a shadow box frame or insert spacers to keep the glass from touching the stitches.

RIBBON EMBROIDERY STITCHES

Some basic embroidery stitches are known by different names, but we have chosen the most commonly used titles, given in alphabetical order. Some flowers use "modified" stitches; these variations are usually described with individual flower instructions.

Unless otherwise directed, bring ribbon up from back to front of fabric at odd (1, 3, 5) numbers and stitch down through fabric at even (2, 4, 6) numbers.

🌸 Backstitch

Bring needle up at 1, a stitch length away from the beginning of an imaginary line. Stitch back down at 2, at beginning of line. Bring needle up at 3, ahead of 1, then stitch back down at 1. Continue, carrying ribbon forward beneath fabric and stitching backward on the surface to cover a curved or straight line.

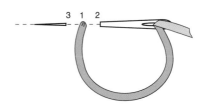

🌸 Braid Stitch

Work a vertical Lazy Daisy Stitch (page 11). Bring needle up one stitch length below at A. Slide needle behind first loop, not piercing the fabric, and stitch down at B, close to A. Pull ribbon to desired shape. Continue in this manner to desired length and end by stitching down at B.

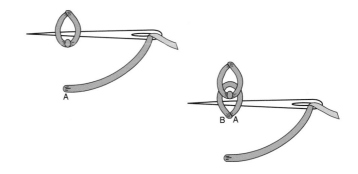

Bullion Lazy Daisy Stitch

Begin as if to make a single link of Chain Stitch (below). Before pulling needle through, loosely wrap ribbon two or three times around pointed end of needle. Gently pull needle through ribbon wrap and fabric, then stitch down to secure loop.

Chain Stitch ❀

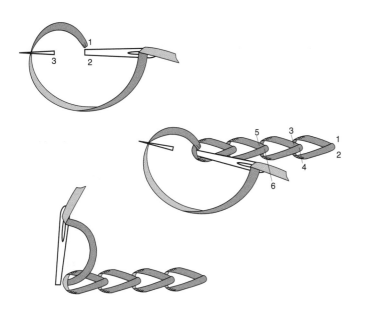

This is a looped stitch with each loop or link being secured to the fabric by the next link. Come up at 1 and swing ribbon in a counterclockwise direction. Straighten any twists and insert needle at 2, one or two threads away from 1 to keep from piercing ribbon. Come up at 3 and pull ribbon through, keeping loop beneath point of needle. Pull until loop is desired fullness. Straighten twists and continue (down at 4 and up at 5) until desired number of loops is completed.

Anchor end of chain by inserting needle over top of loop, close to previous exit point. Chain Stitch can be worked along a straight line or in a circle.

Coral Stitch ❀

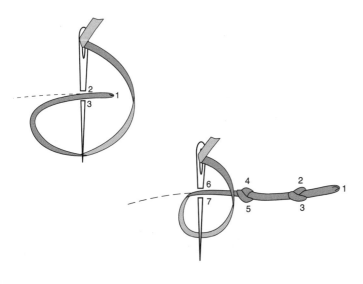

Bring needle up at 1. Straighten ribbon over intended stitching line, then make a counterclockwise loop. Stitch down at 2 and up at 3 with loop below point of needle; pull ribbon through, creating a knot effect. Repeat to reach desired length, flattening ribbon between knots. Stitch down to end desired distance from last knot.

This technique requires two ribbons, one to be flat on the fabric (usually wide) and the other (usually narrow) to hold the first one in place. Bring needle and wide ribbon up at 1, at the left side of area to be covered. Pull ribbon through to the right and park it temporarily at side of fabric.

Use your non-stitching thumb to hold wide ribbon flat as you "couch" it with the other ribbon (or floss). Bring second needle with narrow ribbon up at A, beneath wider ribbon at bottom of first couching point. Pass needle vertically over wider ribbon, and stitch down at top of first couching point at B. Proceed to next couching point. At end of row, pass wider ribbon needle through to back of fabric at 2 and secure it, while holding couched ribbon flat with your thumb to prevent it from folding in on itself.

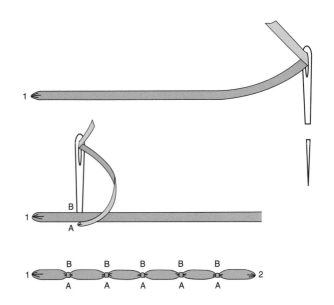

❀ Cretan Stitch

Bring needle up at 1, along an imaginary line. Stitch down at 2 (above the imaginary line) and up at 3 with ribbon beneath point of needle. Pull ribbon through, but do not worry about twists—they will provide textural interest. Swing ribbon below line and stitch down at 4 (below the imaginary line) and up at 5 with ribbon again beneath point. Continue in this manner, with needle always pointing toward line. This stitch can be varied by changing the slope of the stitches or the direction of your work.

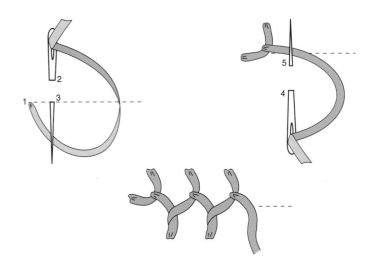

❀ Crossed Chain Stitch

Bring needle up at 1, below intended (dashed) stitching line. Swing ribbon in a counterclockwise direction and stitch down at 2, above intended stitching line. Proceed as for Chain Stitch (page 8), but bring needle up at 3, below stitching line. Continue in this manner, creating a series of wide crossed loops. Anchor end of chain by inserting needle over top of loop, close to previous exit point.

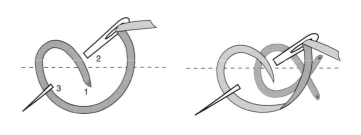

Decorative Lazy Daisy Stitch

Make a Lazy Daisy Stitch (page 11), then work a Straight Stitch (page 15), coming up at A and down at B, inside the open area of the loop.

Detached Crossed Chain Stitch

Begin as if to make a Crossed Chain Stitch (page 9) vertically; end by inserting needle over loop, close to previous exit point.

Extended Fly Stitch

Follow instructions for Fly Stitch (below), lengthening the distance between 3 and 4.

Fishbone Stitch

Begin at the top of the shape. For this stitch, always bring needle up along edge of shape and stitch down toward the center. Work alternating Straight Stitches following the numerical order. Overlap ends of stitches at the center.

Fly Stitch

Bring needle up at 1 and insert at 2; flatten the ribbon as you pull partially through. Bring needle up at 3, making sure loop is below needle. Pull ribbon toward yourself to form a "V" and insert needle at 4 to hold in place.

Thread and knot a small sharp needle with floss or thread to match ribbon and set aside.

Cut an 8" piece of 7mm ribbon. At the center, finger-press a 45-degree fold to create an L-shape (A). Fold and press the horizontal leg to the back so it extends to the left (B). Fold vertical leg to the back so it extends downward (C). Fold the horizontal leg to back so it extends to the right (D), etc. Continue folding each leg in turn, always to the back, alternating directions so the previous fold is secured. When you reach the ends of the ribbon, hold the last fold and its leg firmly between thumb and forefinger, letting the folded section release itself. Pull the other leg gently through the folds. Using the threaded needle, tack base of rose at center and tack rose to background fabric.

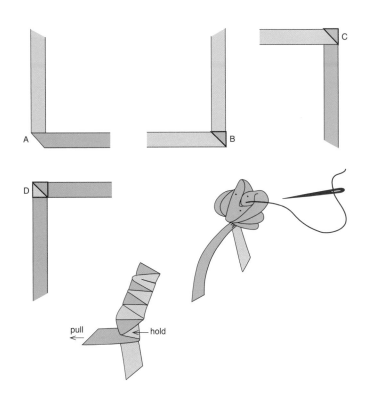

When embroidering with ribbon, French Knots are worked more loosely than with floss or yarn. Bring needle up at 1 and wrap ribbon once or twice (or more times if desired) around shaft of needle. Swing point of needle clockwise and insert into fabric at 2, close to 1. Keep the working ribbon wrapped loosely around needle as you pull needle through to back of fabric. Release wrapping ribbon as knot is formed, and do not pull the knot too tightly. You can change the size of the French Knot by using different ribbon widths, wrapping the ribbon one or more times around needle, and/or varying your tension.

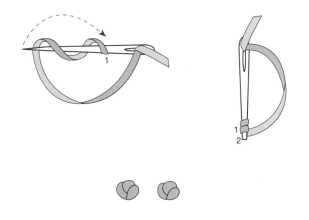

This is actually a single link of Chain Stitch (page 8). Bring needle up at 1 and stitch down at 2, next to 1, skipping a thread or two to avoid piercing the ribbon. Pull until loop is desired length. Bring needle up at 3 with loop below point of needle. Pull ribbon through until desired shape is formed. Re-insert needle over the loop at 4 (close to 3) to anchor it.

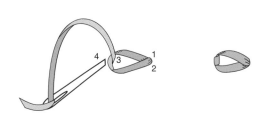

Loop Stitch

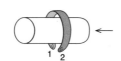

Bring needle up at 1, stitch down at 2 (close to 1), and pull ribbon part way through fabric. Insert a piece of drinking straw (or pencil, large tapestry needle, pin, etc.) through loop; pull ribbon snug to hold shape. Keep straw in place until the next petal is made in the same manner, then remove straw. If desired, these upright petals can be tacked in place.

Padded Ribbon Stitch

Make a short Ribbon Stitch (1-2), page 13, then work a slightly longer Ribbon Stitch (3-4) directly over the first one to create volume.

Padded Straight Stitch

Make a Straight Stitch (page 15), then work a longer Straight Stitch directly over the first one, to create volume.

Pistil Stitch

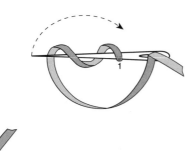

Bring needle up at 1 and wrap ribbon twice around shaft of needle. Swing point of needle clockwise and insert into fabric at 2, a distance from 1. Pull working ribbon wrap around needle; hold wrap with thumb and forefinger of your non-stitching hand, as you pull needle through to back of fabric.

Beginning at top of flower, bring needle up at 1. Stitch down at 2, about ⅛" below 1; untwist and pull ribbon partially through. Insert a holding device, (knitting cable holder, large tapestry needle, pin, etc.) through loop; pull ribbon snug. Hold the device in place with your non-stitching hand, and bring needle up at 3, piercing the base of the loop. Stitch down at 4, ⅛" below 2; move device down into second loop and continue to desired length of shape. To end, stitch back down through base of last loop, to make a tiny tacking stitch.

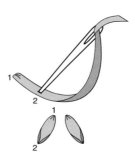

Bring needle up at 1 and flatten ribbon as it emerges through fabric. Extend ribbon just beyond length of stitch and insert needle through top surface of ribbon at 2. Pull ribbon gently through fabric as the sides of ribbon curl inward to form a point. Leave the curls showing by not pulling too tightly. Vary this stitch by using different ribbon widths and tension.

Bring ribbon up at 1 and stitch down at 2 along an imaginary line. Continue in the same manner, making stitches of equal length, equally spaced along the line. Stitch down to end.

Bring needle up at 1 and make a clockwise loop. Stitch down at 2 and up at 3, above and below an imaginary line, with loop below point of needle. Pull through to form a loose knot. Make another clockwise loop then continue in this manner. This stitch can be worked along a straight line, a curve, or in a circle. End by stitching down to hold loop in place.

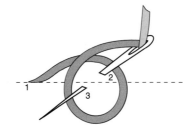

Side Ribbon Stitch

Begin as if for a Ribbon Stitch (page 13), but insert needle close to one edge of ribbon. Continue to gently pull until desired shape for tip is achieved.

Spider Web

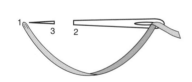

Begin by making an Extended Fly Stitch (page 10) with a narrow ribbon or floss, then add two extra legs (5-6 and 7-8) to create a base. End off ribbon. Bring a different ribbon up at center of web and begin weaving over and under the five legs in a circular manner until desired fullness is achieved. To end, insert needle beneath rose and pull gently through fabric. Do not worry about twists—they add interest and dimension.

Stem Stitch

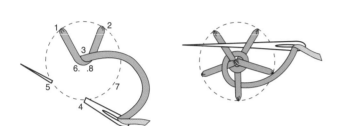

Bring needle up at 1. Use the thumb of your non-stitching hand to hold ribbon flat. Stitch down at 2 and up at 3, then pull the ribbon through. Continue in this manner, with ribbon held below stitching, to make a straight or curved line.

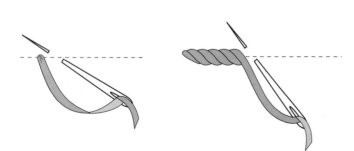

To make a thick Stem Stitch, insert needle slightly below the imaginary line and come up slightly above the line to produce sloping stitches.

Straight Stitch

Bring needle from back of fabric at beginning point of stitch (1). Flatten ribbon with non-stitching thumb beyond intended length of the stitch, and stitch down at opposite end of stitch (2). Pull gently from 1 to 2, while keeping the stitch flat.

Twisted Ribbon Stitch

Begin at 1 as if to make a Ribbon Stitch (page 13), but give the ribbon a single twist to create a point before stitching down at 2.

Twisted Straight Stitch

Bring needle up at 1, give ribbon a single twist, and stitch down at 2.

Whipped Running Stitch

Work one or more Running Stitches (page 13). Bring ribbon back up at A, close to end of last stitch. Wrap by slipping needle once or twice under the Running Stitch. Continue in this manner and stitch down to end.

Wrapped Bar

Make a Straight Stitch (above) of desired length. Bring needle up at A, close to 1. Wrap the bar by slipping needle consecutively several times under the Straight Stitch; wrap to completely fill stitch, and stitch down to end.

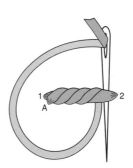

15

RIBBON COLOR CONVERSION KEY

Use this Color Conversion Key as a guide when using different brands of embroidery ribbon. We have listed Bucilla silk, Offray Silk-Ease™, True Colors Silken™, WFR Heirloom Sylk™, and YLI silk ribbons. These five companies have distinct color assortments that may not match each other; the ribbon width selection also varies. These are not complete color range listings for the companies, just for the ribbons used for the flowers in this book. Follow the Stitching Guides for the flowers as you refer to the color photos on pages 17-20 and the back cover, and choose from the array of ribbons that is readily available to you.

For simplicity of description in our stitching guides for the flowers, we have given generic names for the colors with the following abbreviations: lt (light), med (medium) and dk (dark). Refer to the Key for the name of each color used for a flower or motif, then look at the color range of your chosen brand and make adjustments as necessary. These color suggestions will produce similar (but not identical) color schemes as the photographed samples. Occasionally, of necessity, numbers will be repeated; you can choose whether to use the same or a different color value.

	Bucilla	Offray	TC	WFR	YLI		Bucilla	Offray	TC	WFR	YLI
white	003	28	100	558	1	dk yellow	511	660	106	445	54
ivory	655	810	101	470	156	lt yellow-green	509	567	3	419	170
very lt pink	531	117	50	2	5	med yellow-green	642	570	3	374	20
lt pink	544	159	50	4	127	dk yellow-green	653	563	4	364	171
med pink	544	117	40	4	68	very dk yellow-green	653	571	4	366	21
dk pink	553	168	41	13	128	lt bright green	651	550	1	356	94
very dk pink	541	244	51	67	113	med bright green	642	556	3	357	95
lt rose	537	95	50	9	8	very lt green	240	513	1	367	31
med lt rose	540	161	40	34	163	lt green	642	581	3	356	60
med rose	532	140	41	35	112	med green	638	584	5	340	19
dk rose	553	775	23	29	114	dk green	545	580	6	348	61
med red	539	235	20	48	2	lt turquoise	615	530	*302	317	18
dk red	553	169	23	39	129	med turquoise	625	323	*304	336	63
hot pink	552	168	51	18	153	lt aqua	600	316	90	278	10
coral	532	235	41	52	25	med aqua	322	345	80	317	81
med fuchsia	565	178	42	15	145	blue	585	327	80	204	44
dk fuchsia	566	183	43	36	70	lt blue-gray	600	303	90	241	125
very dk fuchsia	566	183	43	39	146	med blue-gray	126	332	80	252	126
very lt peach	531	203	50	23	135	lt purple	009	447	92	182	101
lt peach	514	215	50	102	166	med purple	113	463	93	185	102
very lt orange	514	215	50	102	39	lt orchid	204	434	92	141	22
lt orange	516	707	40	124	106	med orchid	122	430	93	143	23
med orange	516	707	40	124	40	dk orchid	569	467	95	153	84
dk orange	522	745	51	95	43	mauve	571	435	92	175	179
very dk orange	522	753	51	95	41	tan	501	824	101	37	65
med lt yellow	656	640	105	429	119	bronze	668	846	94	136	36
med yellow	666	645	106	424	15	black	002	30	120	600	4

*These colors are variegated ribbons; use the appropriate section of the ribbon.

Anemone

Anthurium

Aster

Baby's Breath

Begonia, Fibrous

Begonia, Tuberous

Bird of Paradise

Bleeding Heart

Bluebells

Buttercup

Calendula

Calla Lily

Camellia

Carnation

Chrysanthemum

Clematis

Columbine

Cone Flower

Cornflower

Cosmos

Crocus

Cyclamen

Daffodil

Dahlia

Daisy

Dogwood

Forget-Me-Not

Forsythia

Foxglove

Fritillaria

Fuchsia

Gazania

Geranium

Gladiolus

Grape
Hyacinth

Hibiscus

Holly

Hollyhock

Hyacinth

Hydrangea

Impatiens

Iris

Larkspur

Lavender   Lilac   Lily   Lily of the Valley

Lupine   Magnolia   Marigold   Mistletoe

Narcissus   Nasturtium   Orchid   Pansy   Peony

Periwinkle   Pine Cone   Poinsettia   Poppy   Primrose

Pussy Willow   Queen Anne's Lace   Red Hot Poker   Rhododendron

Roses

Bradford — Chain Stitch — Coral Stitch — Couched — Crossed Chain Stitch

Fishbone Stitch — Folded Ribbon — Gathered — Loop Stitch — Pin

Ribbon Stitch — Scroll Stitch — Side Ribbon Stitch — Spider Web — Stem Stitch

Rosebuds

Straight Stitch — Wrapped Bar — Bi-Color Straight Stitch — Decorative Lazy Daisy — Detached Twisted Chain — French Knot — Lazy Daisy

Lazy Daisy/ French Knot — Padded Straight Stitch — Ribbon Stitch/ French Knot — Side Ribbon Stitch — Straight Stitch — Straight Stitch/ French Knot

Rose Leaves

Rose Bush

FLOWERS, FOLIAGE, CRITTERS, BOWS

The ribbon flowers are listed alphabetically by common name on pages 20 through 55. The Foliage, Critters, and Bows follow the flowers. The schematic drawing for each design shows the ribbon color and size plus the stitches used for the samples shown on the color pages (17-20) and the back cover. Refer to the key on page 16 for color suggestions using different manufacturers' brands.

Drawing on her botanical background, Deanna has included the Latin name for each flower and the color range in which the flower grows, so you can choose an appropriate color value for your project. Occasionally, additional details and variations are included for your reference. If different ribbon widths or color combinations can be used, this is also noted in the directions.

Six-strand cotton embroidery floss is sometimes used for stems, knots, or small design details. Unless otherwise directed, use two strands of floss. For stems, leaves, and tendrils, choose a color value that complements the foliage. For other design details, refer to the generic color name listed on the schematic and select a color value of your favorite brand of floss.

Anemone (Anemone)

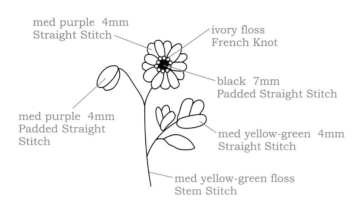

med purple 4mm Straight Stitch

ivory floss French Knot

black 7mm Padded Straight Stitch

med purple 4mm Padded Straight Stitch

med yellow-green 4mm Straight Stitch

med yellow-green floss Stem Stitch

Flower: Work a Padded Straight Stitch (7mm black, yellow, or green) at center. Work up to 14 Straight Stitches (4 or 7mm) around center. Using ivory, black, or yellow floss, surround central stitch with French Knots.

Bud: Work two Padded Straight Stitches (4 or 7mm) to form a spherical bud.

Leaves: Use floss to Stem-Stitch stem. Work groups of three Straight Stitches along stem.

Flower colors: white, cream, yellow, apricot, pink, mauve, rose, lavender, purple

Anthurium (Anthurium)

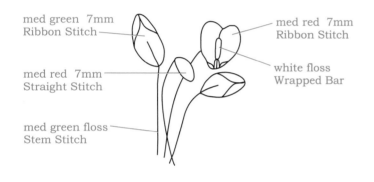

med green 7mm Ribbon Stitch

med red 7mm Ribbon Stitch

white floss Wrapped Bar

med red 7mm Straight Stitch

med green floss Stem Stitch

Flower: Work two Ribbon Stitches with their tips touching to form a heart-shaped base. For the spike, use floss to work a Wrapped Bar on top of base.

Note: Wrapped Bar can be white, yellow, pink or bi-colored (white with yellow or pink wrap).

Bud: Work a short Straight Stitch in same color as flower.

Leaves: Use floss to Stem-Stitch stem. Work a Ribbon Stitch at tip of stem, then continue to Stem-Stitch vein of leaf.

Flower colors: white, pink, red, bi-color (green with red)

Aster (Aster or Callistephus)

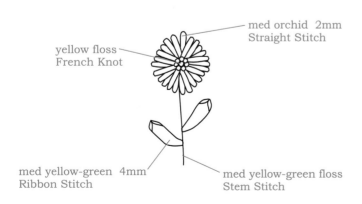

med orchid 2mm Straight Stitch

yellow floss French Knot

med yellow-green 4mm Ribbon Stitch

med yellow-green floss Stem Stitch

Flower: Work 12 -16 Straight Stitches around a small open area. Use yellow floss to fill open area with small French Knots.

Leaves: Use floss to Stem-Stitch stem. Work Ribbon Stitches along stem.

Flower colors: white, cream, pink, rose, violet, violet blue, blue, lavender, purple; China Asters come in white, pink, rose, violet, lavender, blue, purple, crimson, wine, scarlet

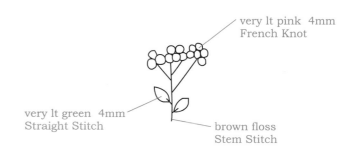

Flower: Use floss to Stem-Stitch the stems. Work clusters of three, four, five, or six French Knots at the end of each stem.

Leaves: Work an occasional Straight Stitch along stem below flower clusters.

Note: This is a "filler plant," occupying the odd or left-over spaces between the main flowers in a floral arrangement.

Flower colors: white, cream, light pink, light rose

very lt pink 4mm
French Knot

very lt green 4mm
Straight Stitch

brown floss
Stem Stitch

Flower: Use floss to Stem-Stitch stem. Work a four-petalled flower of Straight Stitches (4 or 7mm) with two sets of distinctively sized petals (two small and two large) opposite each other. To accomplish the size difference needed, pull the smaller petals tightly and leave the larger petals loose. Use floss (or 2mm ribbon) to work a small French Knot at the center.

Bud: Work a Padded Straight Stitch.

Leaves: Work two Ribbon Stitches with their tips touching to form heart-shaped leaves.

Flower colors: white, salmon, pink, rose, red

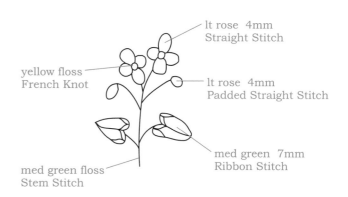

lt rose 4mm
Straight Stitch

yellow floss
French Knot

lt rose 4mm
Padded Straight Stitch

med green 7mm
Ribbon Stitch

med green floss
Stem Stitch

Flower: Work a large compound flower with three concentric circles of loose Straight Stitches. Begin at the outside edge; make petals smaller toward the center.

Bud: Work two overlapping Padded Straight Stitches to resemble a small clam shell. Using floss, work a French Knot at center top of bud where bud stem ends.

Leaves: Use floss to Stem-Stitch stem. Work leaves as for Fibrous Begonia above.

Flower colors: white, yellow, apricot, salmon, orange, pink, rose, red, bi-color

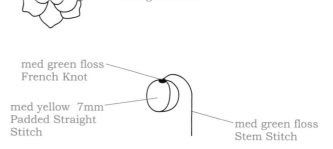

med yellow 7mm
Straight Stitch

med green floss
French Knot

med yellow 7mm
Padded Straight
Stitch

med green floss
Stem Stitch

Bird of Paradise 🌺 (Strelitzia)

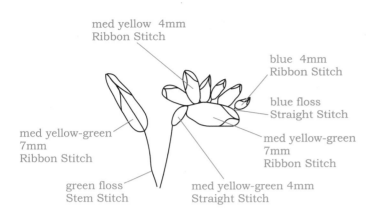

med yellow 4mm
Ribbon Stitch

blue 4mm
Ribbon Stitch

blue floss
Straight Stitch

med yellow-green
7mm
Ribbon Stitch

med yellow-green
7mm
Ribbon Stitch

green floss
Stem Stitch

med yellow-green 4mm
Straight Stitch

Flower: Work the main body with one large Ribbon Stitch. Fanning across top edge of body, make large yellow Ribbon Stitches interspersed with smaller blue Ribbon Stitches having short Straight-Stitched blue stems. Add a Straight Stitch to the stem side (non-pointed end) of the body.

Leaves: Work a thick stalk with Stem Stitch. At the tip of the stalk, make a Ribbon Stitch. Stem-Stitch the vein with floss.

Flower colors: yellow-gold, orange, or pink with periwinkle blue

Bleeding Heart 🌺 (Dicentra)

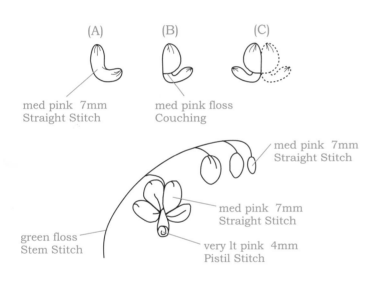

(A)

(B)

(C)

med pink 7mm
Straight Stitch

med pink floss
Couching

med pink 7mm
Straight Stitch

med pink 7mm
Straight Stitch

green floss
Stem Stitch

very lt pink 4mm
Pistil Stitch

Flower: Stitch two **loose** Straight Stitches (4 or 7mm) to form back-to-back L-shapes (A, B, C); using floss to match ribbon, couch at bend of each "L". Work one Pistil Stitch downward from couching. Stem-Stitch branch and stems with floss.

Bud: Straight Stitch each bud at top of stem.

Note: Each floral spray usually has two or three full flowers at the base with two or three short buds along the branch, gradually decreasing in size towards tip.

Leaves: Work short Straight Stitches in desired shade of green.

Flower colors: rose pink (light or dark), cream

Bluebell 🌺 (Campanula)

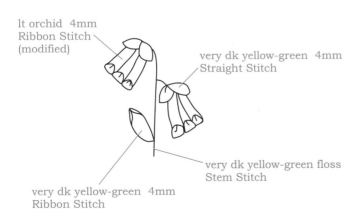

lt orchid 4mm
Ribbon Stitch
(modified)

very dk yellow-green 4mm
Straight Stitch

very dk yellow-green floss
Stem Stitch

very dk yellow-green 4mm
Ribbon Stitch

Flower: Work three modified Ribbon Stitches (4 or 7mm) for each flower, pulling the ribbon only until a "roll" appears at the end of the stitch. If pulled too tightly, the usual curves will appear at the end instead of the roll. To form the calyx, work two Straight Stitches at base of each flower.

Leaves: Use floss to Stem-Stitch stem. Work alternate Ribbon Stitches (4 or 7mm), along stem.

Flower colors: white, pink, magenta, blue, lavender, purple

Flower: Method A—Work five short loose Straight-Stitched petals (4 or 7mm) in a circle. At the center, make a French Knot and surround it with Pistil Stitches worked with floss (one or two per petal).
Method B—Work five Loop-Stitched petals (4 or 7mm) in a circle. At the center work a cluster of French Knots.
Leaves: Work three Straight Stitches (4 or 7mm) with the center stitch on top. Stem-Stitch the vein and stem with floss.
Flower color: yellow

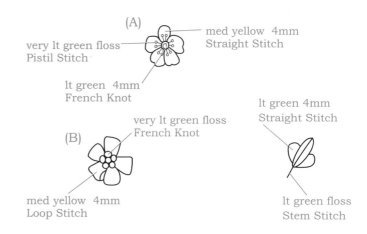

(A)
very lt green floss Pistil Stitch
med yellow 4mm Straight Stitch
lt green 4mm French Knot

(B)
very lt green floss French Knot
med yellow 4mm Loop Stitch
lt green 4mm Straight Stitch
lt green floss Stem Stitch

Flower: Work two concentric circles of Straight Stitches (2 or 4mm) around a center opening. Work the outer circle first with eight pairs (16 total) of stitches. Then do the inner circle, working slightly shorter Straight Stitches between outer petals, always entering fabric close to center. For a side view, work Straight Stitches radiating from base with center stitch on top.
Leaves: Work Ribbon Stitch (4 or 7mm) alternately along Stem-Stitched stem.
Flower colors: yellow, gold, apricot, orange

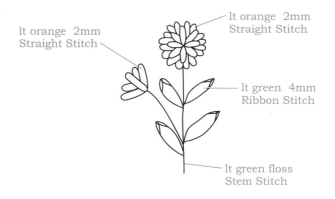

lt orange 2mm Straight Stitch
lt orange 2mm Straight Stitch
lt green 4mm Ribbon Stitch
lt green floss Stem Stitch

Flower: Make a modified Lazy Daisy Stitch. Bring needle up and stitch back down at base of flower; pull through only until folds form on each side. Bring right-side fold over left side. Use ivory floss to tack folds to fabric; the usual ribbon tack-down stitch is omitted. Work a Wrapped Bar within the fold on lower half of flower.
Leaves: Work two Side Ribbon Stitches (4 or 7mm) together with a Stem-Stitched stem continuing into the leaf.
Flower colors: white, yellow, pink

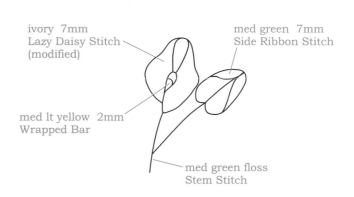

ivory 7mm Lazy Daisy Stitch (modified)
med green 7mm Side Ribbon Stitch
med lt yellow 2mm Wrapped Bar
med green floss Stem Stitch

Camellia 🌸 (Camellia)

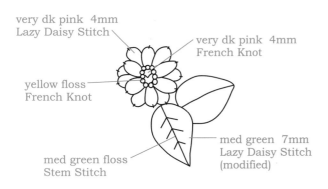

very dk pink 4mm
Lazy Daisy Stitch

very dk pink 4mm
French Knot

yellow floss
French Knot

med green floss
Stem Stitch

med green 7mm
Lazy Daisy Stitch
(modified)

Flower: Work two concentric circles of Lazy Daisy Stitches around a small open area. Work a matching French Knot at center. Use floss to surround center with French Knots.

Leaves: Thread needle with floss to match leaf and set aside. Work a modified Lazy Daisy Stitch. Bring needle up and stitch back down at base of leaf; pull through only until folds form beneath tip. Omit the tack-down stitch. Hold (or pin) leaf in place and Stem-Stitch the vein with pre-threaded needle.

Flower colors: white, all shades of pink, salmon, red

Carnation 🌸 (Dianthus)

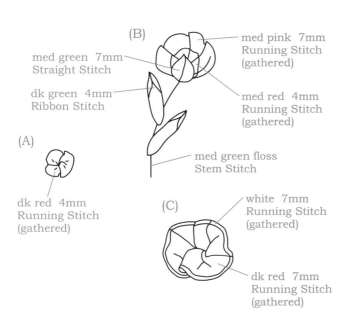

(B)

med green 7mm
Straight Stitch

dk green 4mm
Ribbon Stitch

med pink 7mm
Running Stitch
(gathered)

med red 4mm
Running Stitch
(gathered)

(A)

dk red 4mm
Running Stitch
(gathered)

(C)

med green floss
Stem Stitch

white 7mm
Running Stitch
(gathered)

dk red 7mm
Running Stitch
(gathered)

Flower: Method A—Cut a 2" piece of 4mm ribbon. Using floss to match ribbon, work Running Stitch along one long edge of the ribbon; pull to gather into a tight circle. Turn under raw ends and tack to fabric.

Method B—Cut one 3" piece each of 7mm and 4mm ribbons. With narrow ribbon on top and long edges aligned on one side, gather the two layers together as for Method A and tack to fabric. To form calyx, work two overlapping Straight Stitches. Method C—Cut one 3" piece each of two 7mm ribbons. Place one over the other with long edges aligned, and gather and tack as for Method A.

Note: To make a side view, gather only a half circle.

Leaves: Work Ribbon Stitch over a stem that is Stem-Stitched with floss.

Flower colors: white, pink, red, magenta, maroon, yellow, apricot, orange, and bi-color (usually white with any of the previous colors)

Chrysanthemum 🌸 (Chrysanthemum)

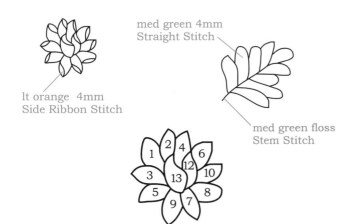

med green 4mm
Straight Stitch

lt orange 4mm
Side Ribbon Stitch

med green floss
Stem Stitch

Flower: Work Side Ribbon Stitch in the numerical sequence shown in the enlarged drawing. The #11 stitch is worked directly beneath the #13 stitch to give a padded effect.

Leaves: Use floss to Stem-Stitch the stem, then work Straight Stitches opposite each other, decreasing size toward end of branch.

Flower colors: white, yellow, bronze, pink, magenta, maroon, orange, gold, salmon, lavender

Flower: The petals can be stitched in two ways. Work six, seven, or eight Lazy Daisy or Decorative Lazy Daisy Stitches (or a combination of both) around a small open circle. Work a French Knot (2 or 4mm ribbon or floss) in central open area. Work Straight Stitches (one per petal and one between petals) radiating from knot.

Leaves: Work a Straight Stitch at the end of a stem that is Stem-Stitched with floss.

Flower colors: white, pink, magenta, purple, blue, yellow, and bi-color (often white combined with one of the previous colors)

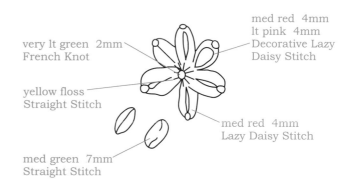

very lt green 2mm French Knot

yellow floss Straight Stitch

med green 7mm Straight Stitch

med red 4mm
lt pink 4mm
Decorative Lazy Daisy Stitch

med red 4mm Lazy Daisy Stitch

(Aquilegia) 🌸 *Columbine*

Flower: Work two modified Ribbon Stitches, pulling the ribbon only until a "roll" appears at the end of the stitch. If pulled too tightly, the usual curves will appear at the end instead of the roll. Above them work three Lazy Daisy Stitches. Extending behind the upper portion of the flower, work Bullion Lazy Daisies; below the flower use floss to work three Pistil Stitches.

Leaves: Work three short Straight Stitches, one on each side and the center one on top, at the ends of Stem-Stitched stems.

Flower colors: lower (inner) petals—white, cream, yellow; upper (outer) petals—white, cream, yellow, blue, lavender, purple, red, rose

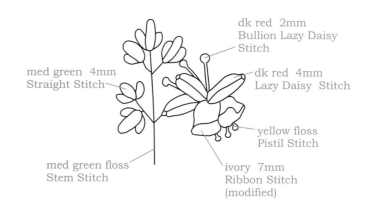

med green 4mm Straight Stitch

med green floss Stem Stitch

dk red 2mm Bullion Lazy Daisy Stitch

dk red 4mm Lazy Daisy Stitch

yellow floss Pistil Stitch

ivory 7mm Ribbon Stitch (modified)

(Ratibida) 🌸 *Cone Flower*

Flower: Work a truncated cone of French Knots, gradually changing the color from dark brown at the base to medium brown at the tip. Make a cluster of five Straight Stitches radiating from base of French Knots.

Leaves: Work alternating Straight Stitches along the Stem-Stitched stalk.

Flower colors: yellow, orange

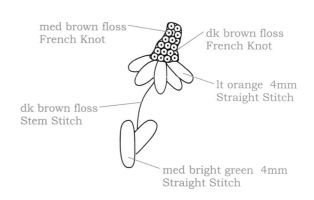

med brown floss French Knot

dk brown floss French Knot

lt orange 4mm Straight Stitch

dk brown floss Stem Stitch

med bright green 4mm Straight Stitch

Cornflower (Centaurea)

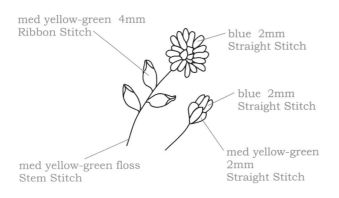

med yellow-green 4mm Ribbon Stitch

blue 2mm Straight Stitch

blue 2mm Straight Stitch

med yellow-green floss Stem Stitch

med yellow-green 2mm Straight Stitch

Flower: Work two concentric circles of Straight Stitches around a small open area. Make the inner circle of stitches shorter than the outer circle. Stitch very short Straight Stitches to cover the open central area.

Bud: Work three Straight Stitches with three overlapping short Straight Stitches at base.

Leaves: Work Ribbon Stitches alternating along a Stem-Stitched stem.

Flower colors: white, blue, pink, maroon

Cosmos (Cosmos)

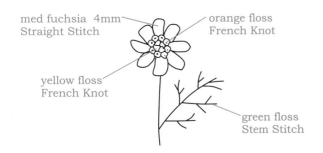

med fuchsia 4mm Straight Stitch

orange floss French Knot

yellow floss French Knot

green floss Stem Stitch

Flower: Work eight Straight Stitches (4 or 7mm) around an open central area. Using floss, work a French Knot at base of each petal. Fill the remaining open center with tiny French Knots of a lighter color value.

Leaves: Stem-Stitch the finely dissected leaves and stem with floss.

Flower colors: white, yellow, orange, pink, rose, crimson

Crocus (Crocus)

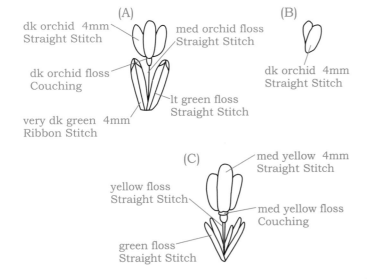

(A)

dk orchid 4mm Straight Stitch

med orchid floss Straight Stitch

dk orchid floss Couching

lt green floss Straight Stitch

very dk green 4mm Ribbon Stitch

(B)

dk orchid 4mm Straight Stitch

(C)

med yellow 4mm Straight Stitch

yellow floss Straight Stitch

med yellow floss Couching

green floss Straight Stitch

Flower: (A or C) Work three Straight Stitches (4 or 7mm); make the side stitches first, then a longer center stitch that extends above and below the side stitches. Use matching floss to Couch base of center petal, squeezing base of petal. Use three or four strands of floss to make a long Straight Stitch for stem.

Bud: (B) Work two overlapping Straight Stitches (4 or 7mm).

Leaves: For large leaves (A), work Ribbon Stitches; Straight-Stitch vein with floss. For small leaves (C), work Straight Stitches (floss or 2mm ribbon).

Flower colors: white, cream, yellow, lavender, medium and dark purple

Flower: Method A—Work three Straight Stitches (4 or 7mm); make side stitches first, then center stitch on top. Use yellow floss to stitch two short Straight Stitches across base of petals. Method B—Begin as in Method A, but use a contrasting color of floss to stitch three short Straight Stitches radiating from base of petals.
Leaves: Work two Straight Stitches (4 or 7mm) so the tips meet and the leaf resembles a heart. Use floss to Stem-Stitch vein and stems. For a variation (C)—Work two Side Ribbon Stitches.
Flower colors: white, pink, magenta, rose, red, salmon

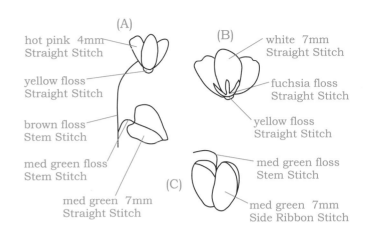

(A)
hot pink 4mm Straight Stitch
yellow floss Straight Stitch
brown floss Stem Stitch
med green floss Stem Stitch
med green 7mm Straight Stitch

(B)
white 7mm Straight Stitch
fuchsia floss Straight Stitch
yellow floss Straight Stitch

(C)
med green floss Stem Stitch
med green 7mm Side Ribbon Stitch

Flower: Method A—Make one Loop Stitch (4 or 7mm) for the trumpet portion of the flower; use floss to work three Straight Stitches radiating from base of Loop Stitch. With matching floss, tack back of Loop Stitch to fabric. Straight-Stitch the stem with floss, tacking bend in desired position.
Method B—Work five overlapping Straight Stitches for petals; work a Loop Stitch for trumpet. With matching floss, tack back of Loop Stitch to fabric.
Method C—Work a Loop Stitch for trumpet; make three overlapping Straight Stitches covering base of trumpet.
Leaves: Work a loose, Twisted Straight Stitch. Bend ribbon leaf as desired and tack with matching floss to preserve bend.
Flower colors: trumpet—white, cream, light or dark yellow, orange, apricot; petals—white, cream, yellow

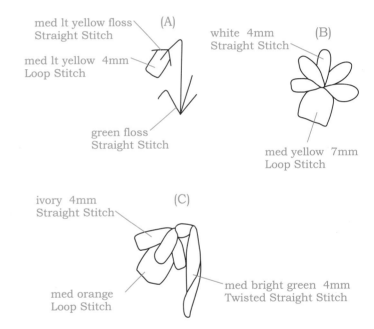

(A)
med lt yellow floss Straight Stitch
med lt yellow 4mm Loop Stitch
green floss Straight Stitch

(B)
white 4mm Straight Stitch
med yellow 7mm Loop Stitch

(C)
ivory 4mm Straight Stitch
med orange Loop Stitch
med bright green 4mm Twisted Straight Stitch

Flower: Work two concentric circles of Ribbon Stitches (4 or 7mm) with no open center area. Work the outer circle first; make the inner ring slightly shorter than the outer circle.
Leaves: Stem-Stitch leaf stem with floss. Work three Straight Stitches (4 or 7mm) with bases sharing a point, as for Trillium, page 54.
Flower colors: white, yellow, apricot, orange, pink, rose, magenta, red

dk rose 7mm Ribbon Stitch

Daisy 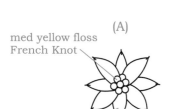 *(Chrysanthemum, Rudbeckia, Emilia and others)*

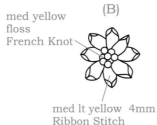

(A)
med yellow floss
French Knot

dk pink 4mm
Bullion Lazy Daisy
Stitch

(B)
med yellow
floss
French Knot

med lt yellow 4mm
Ribbon Stitch

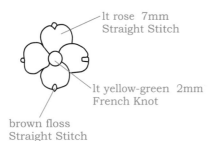

(C)
white 4mm
Loop Stitch

med yellow 2mm
French Knot

(D)
med yellow
floss
French Knot

lt blue-gray 2mm
Straight Stitch

Flower: We show four ways to make petals around a small central opening. After stitching the petals, fill centers of all daisies with French Knots (2 or 4mm).
Method A—Work eight evenly spaced Bullion Lazy Daisy Stitches.
Method B—Work eight evenly spaced Ribbon Stitches.
Method C—Work six or more Loop Stitches (2 or 4mm).
Method D—Work two concentric circles of Straight Stitches with the inner row covering the spaces between the outer row of stitches.
Leaves: Work Straight or Ribbon Stitches alternating along a Stem-Stitched flower stem.
Flower colors: petals—white, light and dark yellow, apricot, pink, rose; center—yellow, orange, brown

Dogwood  *(Cornus)*

med green 7mm
Ribbon Stitch

dk green floss
Stem Stitch

lt rose 7mm
Straight Stitch

lt yellow-green 2mm
French Knot

brown floss
Straight Stitch

Flower: Work four loose Straight Stitches around a small open area. Use floss to tack down the end of each Straight Stitch. Fill the central open area with small French Knots (floss or 2mm).
Leaves: Work Ribbon Stitch and use floss to Stem-Stitch stem and vein.
Flower colors: white, cream, light yellow-green, pink, rose

Forget-Me-Not 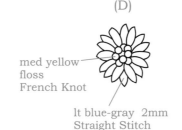 *(Myosotis)*

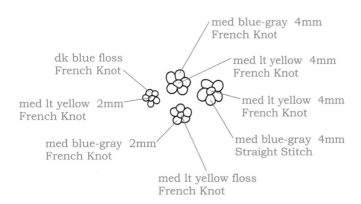

med blue-gray 4mm
French Knot

dk blue floss
French Knot

med lt yellow 4mm
French Knot

med lt yellow 2mm
French Knot

med lt yellow 4mm
French Knot

med blue-gray 2mm
French Knot

med blue-gray 4mm
Straight Stitch

med lt yellow floss
French Knot

Flower: Work five French Knots or Straight Stitches (2 or 4mm) in a circle. Work a single yellow (or white) French Knot (2 or 4mm or floss) at center.
Leaves: Work short Straight or Ribbon Stitches (2 or 4mm) at base of flower and scattered along a Stem-Stitched stem.
Flower colors: white, pink, rose, blue

Flower: For the open blossom, work four yellow Twisted Ribbon Stitches. Work a lighter yellow French Knot at center.
Note: Gradually decrease the size and openness of flowers as they proceed to the tip of the branch.
Bud: For a partially opened bud, work one to three Twisted Ribbon Stitches with a small short green Straight Stitch at base. For an unopened bud, work a green Straight Stitch.
Leaves: Use floss to Stem-Stitch stem. Work Ribbon Stitches along stem.
Flower colors: light to bright yellow

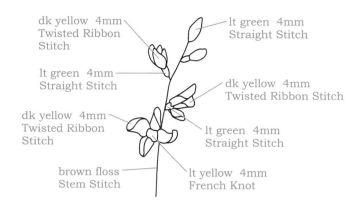

dk yellow 4mm Twisted Ribbon Stitch

lt green 4mm Straight Stitch

lt green 4mm Straight Stitch

dk yellow 4mm Twisted Ribbon Stitch

dk yellow 4mm Twisted Ribbon Stitch

lt green 4mm Straight Stitch

brown floss Stem Stitch

lt yellow 4mm French Knot

Note: This plant has a tall flower stalk of increasingly mature flowers from the tip downwards. Begin working buds at the tip.
Bud: Work increasing sizes of French Knots, the top ones being green, and the lower ones changing to match flower color.
Flower: Work mid-sized flowers with Straight Stitches (4 or 7mm) and largest flowers with Ribbon Stitch (4 or 7mm).
Leaves: Use floss to Stem-Stitch stem. Work Straight Stitches (4 or 7mm) along stem.
Flower colors: white, yellow, apricot, salmon, pink, magenta, plum, purple

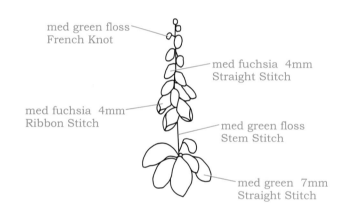

med green floss French Knot

med fuchsia 4mm Straight Stitch

med fuchsia 4mm Ribbon Stitch

med green floss Stem Stitch

med green 7mm Straight Stitch

Flower: Work three Straight Stitches; make the center stitch first, then the side stitches, overlapping in a consistent manner.
Leaves: Use floss to Stem-Stitch stem. Work Straight Stitches in desired locations. For bent leaves, bring needle and ribbon up at base of leaf. Use matching floss to Couch ribbon to fabric at desired bending point, fold ribbon over couching thread, then complete the stitch.
Note: For some species the leaves are clustered at base, while others alternate along flower stalk.
Flower colors: white, yellow, pink, plum, purple

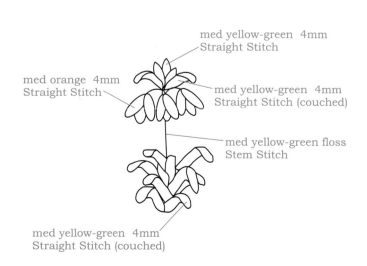

med yellow-green 4mm Straight Stitch

med orange 4mm Straight Stitch

med yellow-green 4mm Straight Stitch (couched)

med yellow-green floss Stem Stitch

med yellow-green 4mm Straight Stitch (couched)

Fuchsia ❀ *(Fuchsia)*

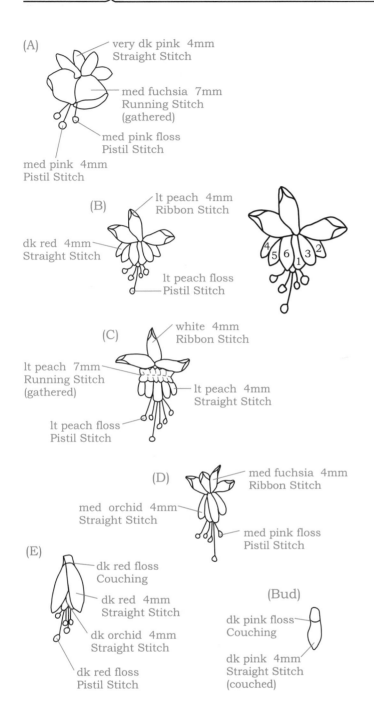

(A)
- very dk pink 4mm Straight Stitch
- med fuchsia 7mm Running Stitch (gathered)
- med pink floss Pistil Stitch
- med pink 4mm Pistil Stitch

(B)
- lt peach 4mm Ribbon Stitch
- dk red 4mm Straight Stitch
- lt peach floss Pistil Stitch

4 5 6 1 3 2

(C)
- white 4mm Ribbon Stitch
- lt peach 7mm Running Stitch (gathered)
- lt peach 4mm Straight Stitch
- lt peach floss Pistil Stitch

(D)
- med fuchsia 4mm Ribbon Stitch
- med orchid 4mm Straight Stitch
- med pink floss Pistil Stitch

(E)
- dk red floss Couching
- dk red 4mm Straight Stitch
- dk orchid 4mm Straight Stitch
- dk red floss Pistil Stitch

(Bud)
- dk pink floss Couching
- dk pink 4mm Straight Stitch (couched)

Notes: We show five ways to make the blossoms. The calyx is the group of upper petals, and the corolla is the lower group of petals, which may be individual petals or formed into a tube shape. For most variations, use floss to work pistil and stamen with Pistil Stitches.

Flower: Method A—Make the calyx first by working four Straight Stitches. Cut a 2" piece of 7mm ribbon for the corolla, and use matching floss to work Running Stitches along one edge. Pull floss to gather tightly; hide raw ends at back and tack to fabric. Work Pistil Stitches from center of gathered shape so they extend below corolla.

Method B—Work corolla first with Straight Stitches. Follow the numerical sequence shown in the enlarged drawing. Work three Ribbon Stitches for calyx, covering base of corolla.

Method C—Make the lower part of the calyx with five Straight Stitches ending at center. Make the upper part by cutting a 1" piece of 7mm ribbon, and use matching floss to work Running Stitches lengthwise through middle of ribbon. Pull floss to gather and turn raw ends under; tack above Straight Stitches. Work three Ribbon Stitches radiating from center top of gathering.

Method D—Work four Ribbon Stitches to form calyx. For the corolla, work overlapping Straight Stitches beginning at each outside edge so the topmost stitch is close to center.

Method E—This partially closed blossom has the calyx covering most of the corolla. Work two overlapping Straight Stitches for the corolla. Work two overlapping Straight Stitches for the calyx, covering all but center portion of corolla. Use matching floss to Couch across top of stitch.

Bud: Work a Straight Stitch (4 or 7mm). Use matching floss to Couch across top of stitch.

Leaves: Work Ribbon or Straight Stitches on a branch that is Stem-Stitched with floss.

Flower colors: calyx—white, light pink, rose, magenta, apricot; corolla—white, pink, rose, purple, salmon

Gazania ❀ *(Gazania)*

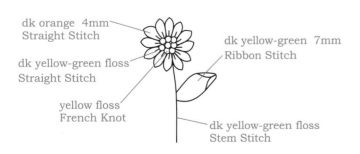

- dk orange 4mm Straight Stitch
- dk yellow-green floss Straight Stitch
- yellow floss French Knot
- dk yellow-green 7mm Ribbon Stitch
- dk yellow-green floss Stem Stitch

Flower: Work Straight Stitches around a central open area. Use floss to fill the open area with French Knots. At the base of each petal work a Straight Stitch with floss.

Leaves: Work Ribbon Stitches along a stem that is Stem-Stitched with floss.

Flower colors: yellow, orange, red-orange, rose

Flower: Work a circular cluster of loose French Knots.
Leaves: Work two short, loose Straight Stitches with tips sharing the same hole. Use floss to Stem-Stitch the stems.
Flower colors: white, apricot, salmon, pink, magenta, red

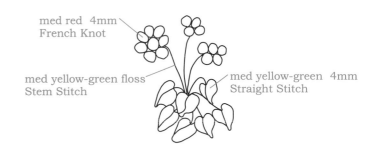

med red 4mm
French Knot

med yellow-green floss
Stem Stitch

med yellow-green 4mm
Straight Stitch

Flower: Work two concentric circles of three Straight or modified Lazy Daisy Stitches. Work the three lower ones first then the three upper ones in between the first petals and with centers touching. For the modified stitches, only the loops of the Lazy Daisy Stitches are formed with the ribbon; use matching floss to make the tack-down portion of each stitch and to tack down the outer point of each petal. In the center of the flower work three Pistil Stitches with floss.
Bud: Work two Straight Stitches, one partially overlapping the other. The topmost stitch is the flower color and the overlapping stitch is green.
Leaves: Work long Twisted Straight Stitches; use matching floss to tack twist in place if needed.
Flower colors: white, yellow, apricot, salmon, coral, orange, pink, rose, magenta, red, lavender, purple, bi-color

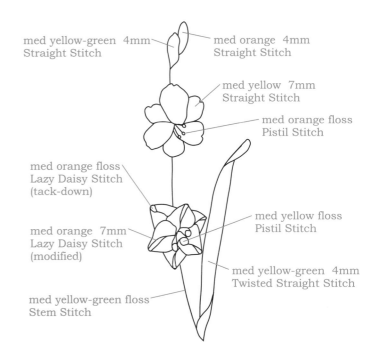

med yellow-green 4mm
Straight Stitch

med orange 4mm
Straight Stitch

med yellow 7mm
Straight Stitch

med orange floss
Pistil Stitch

med orange floss
Lazy Daisy Stitch
(tack-down)

med yellow floss
Pistil Stitch

med orange 7mm
Lazy Daisy Stitch
(modified)

med yellow-green 4mm
Twisted Straight Stitch

med yellow-green floss
Stem Stitch

Flower: Work a cone shaped cluster of French Knots with large knots at the base of the cone, gradually becoming smaller toward tip of cone.
Leaves: Work Straight Stitches (2mm ribbon or floss). A few leaves can be bent and couched in place.
Flower colors: white, violet, blue, light and dark blue-purple

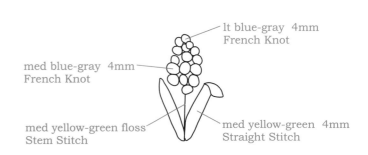

lt blue-gray 4mm
French Knot

med blue-gray 4mm
French Knot

med yellow-green floss
Stem Stitch

med yellow-green 4mm
Straight Stitch

Hibiscus ❋ (Hibiscus)

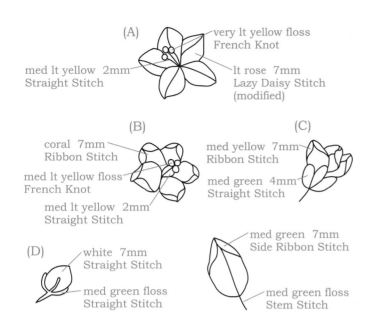

(A)

very lt yellow floss
French Knot

med lt yellow 2mm
Straight Stitch

lt rose 7mm
Lazy Daisy Stitch
(modified)

(B)

coral 7mm
Ribbon Stitch

med lt yellow floss
French Knot

med lt yellow 2mm
Straight Stitch

(C)

med yellow 7mm
Ribbon Stitch

med green 4mm
Straight Stitch

(D)

white 7mm
Straight Stitch

med green floss
Straight Stitch

med green 7mm
Side Ribbon Stitch

med green floss
Stem Stitch

Flower: Work five modified Lazy Daisy Stitches (A) or Ribbon Stitches (B), leaving a small open central area. For the modified stitches, only the loops of the Lazy Daisy Stitches are formed with ribbon; use matching floss to make the tack-down portion of the stitch. At the center, work three Straight Stitches using floss to work a French Knot at the tip of each.

Buds: For an open bud (C), work two or three Ribbon Stitches with three Straight Stitches at their base. For a closed bud (D), work one Straight Stitch with three Straight Stitches (2mm or floss) overlapping the base.

Leaves: Work two Side Ribbon Stitches with bases and tips touching and a Stem-Stitched stem and vein.

Flower colors: white, yellow, apricot, salmon, orange, pink, rose, magenta, red, purple, bi-color

Holly ❋ (Ilex)

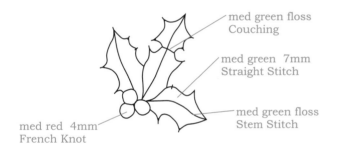

med green floss
Couching

med green 7mm
Straight Stitch

med green floss
Stem Stitch

med red 4mm
French Knot

Berries: Work loose two-wrap French Knots.

Leaves: Work a straight or loose curving Straight Stitch (4 or 7mm). Use matching floss to work short Straight Stitches to form vein and the marginal spines. For the long middle leaf, use matching floss to Couch across upper third of leaf, pinching in sides of ribbon.

Berry colors: yellow, orange, red

Hollyhock ❋ (Alcea)

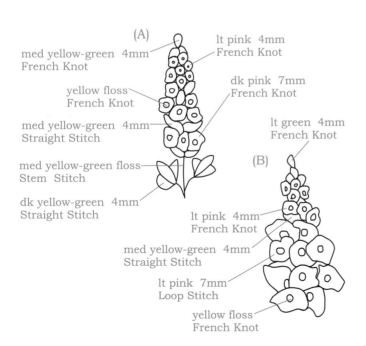

(A)

med yellow-green 4mm
French Knot

lt pink 4mm
French Knot

yellow floss
French Knot

dk pink 7mm
French Knot

med yellow-green 4mm
Straight Stitch

lt green 4mm
French Knot

med yellow-green floss
Stem Stitch

(B)

dk yellow-green 4mm
Straight Stitch

lt pink 4mm
French Knot

med yellow-green 4mm
Straight Stitch

lt pink 7mm
Loop Stitch

yellow floss
French Knot

Flower: Work a cone-shaped cluster of blossoms. Begin working at the top with a few green French Knots. Change to the flower color and work increasingly larger French Knots toward the base (A); double-wrap and/or loosen the knots to increase their size. Use floss to anchor center of each large blossom with a French Knot. For a variation (B), work loose Loop Stitches toward the base; to flatten each loop, use floss to anchor center with a French Knot.

Leaves: For the small leaves interspersed among the flowers, work single Straight Stitches. For the larger leaves below the flowers, work three Straight Stitches, fanning out from a common base with the longer middle stitch on top. Stem Stitch the stem with floss.

Flower colors: white, yellow, apricot, pink, rose, red, purple

Flower: Work five loose Straight or Twisted Straight Stitches (2 or 4mm), leaving a small open central area. At center, work a French Knot (floss or 2 or 4mm ribbon) with matching color. Work a thick stem with Stem Stitch.
Leaves: Work long Twisted Straight Stitches.
Flower colors: white, yellow, salmon, pink, rose, red, violet, blue, purple

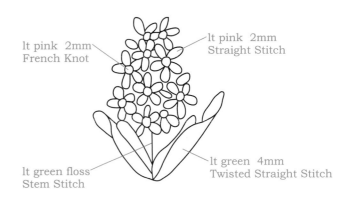

lt pink 2mm
French Knot

lt pink 2mm
Straight Stitch

lt green floss
Stem Stitch

lt green 4mm
Twisted Straight Stitch

Flower: For the large single blossom, work four Straight Stitches with a French Knot at center. Use floss to work a Straight Stitch at base of each petal. For the large flower head, work the lower two-thirds as individual blossoms with four Straight Stitches and a central French Knot. Occasionally work a Straight Stitch between the four-petalled flowers to fill in the flower head. Work the top third of the flower head with French Knots.
Note: For lace-top varieties, stitch a flattened circle of two to four-petalled flowers around the periphery with French Knots in the center of the flower head.
Leaves: Work one Straight Stitch for length of leaf. Directly over it, work two Ribbon Stitches so the tips of all three stitches meet at a single point at each end. Stem-Stitch the veins and stem with floss.
Flower colors: white, pink, rose, maroon, blue

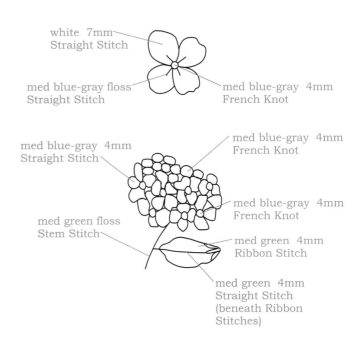

white 7mm
Straight Stitch

med blue-gray floss
Straight Stitch

med blue-gray 4mm
French Knot

med blue-gray 4mm
Straight Stitch

med blue-gray 4mm
French Knot

med green floss
Stem Stitch

med blue-gray 4mm
French Knot

med green 4mm
Ribbon Stitch

med green 4mm
Straight Stitch
(beneath Ribbon
Stitches)

Note: Work leaves first, then petals.
Leaves: Work Ribbon Stitches around a large central opening.
Flower: Work six loose Straight Stitches (4 or 7mm) around a central point. Two of the petals should be opposite each other and on top of the other petals. Work a French Knot (2 or 4mm) at center. Use floss to work Straight Stitches.
Bud: Work short, loose Padded Ribbon Stitches.
Flower colors: white, blush, salmon, orange, pink, rose, cranberry, red, violet, blue

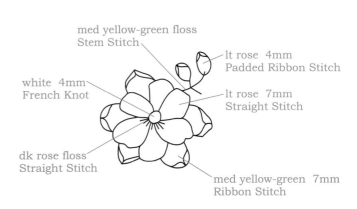

med yellow-green floss
Stem Stitch

lt rose 4mm
Padded Ribbon Stitch

white 4mm
French Knot

lt rose 7mm
Straight Stitch

dk rose floss
Straight Stitch

med yellow-green 7mm
Ribbon Stitch

35

Iris (Iris)

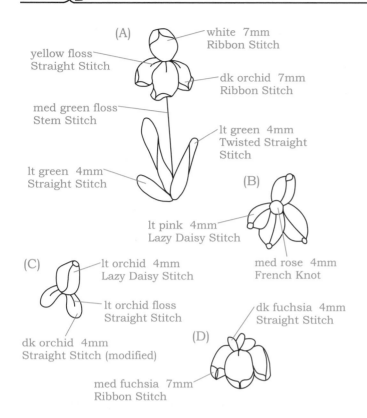

(A)
yellow floss
Straight Stitch

white 7mm
Ribbon Stitch

dk orchid 7mm
Ribbon Stitch

med green floss
Stem Stitch

lt green 4mm
Twisted Straight
Stitch

lt green 4mm
Straight Stitch

(B)

lt pink 4mm
Lazy Daisy Stitch

(C)
lt orchid 4mm
Lazy Daisy Stitch

med rose 4mm
French Knot

lt orchid floss
Straight Stitch

dk fuchsia 4mm
Straight Stitch

(D)

dk orchid 4mm
Straight Stitch (modified)

med fuchsia 7mm
Ribbon Stitch

Flower: We show four ways to make an iris blossom. The upright petals are called standards and the lower petals are called falls.
Method A—Work one Ribbon Stitch (4 or 7mm) for the standard and three Ribbon Stitches for the falls. Use floss to Straight-Stitch the beard on each fall. Use floss to Stem-Stitch the stem.
Method B—Work Lazy Daisy Stitches (2, 4 or 7mm) for the standard and falls. Work a French Knot at center.
Method C—Work a Lazy Daisy Stitch (4 or 7mm) for the standard. Work a modified Straight Stitch (4 or 7mm) for the falls. Bring ribbon up at intended bottom tip of right side fall; slip needle beneath base of standard, not entering fabric, and stitch down at tip of left-side fall.
Method D (Japanese Iris)—Work three short Straight Stitches (2 or 4mm) for the standards and three overlapping Ribbon Stitches (4 or 7mm) for the falls.
Leaves: Work Straight or Twisted Straight Stitches.
Flower colors: white, yellow, apricot, salmon, bronze, gold, copper, pink, rose, lavender, violet, blue, purple, bi-color of most of the above colors

Larkspur (Delphinium)

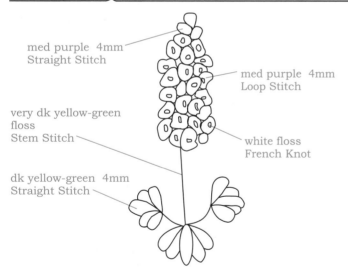

med purple 4mm
Straight Stitch

med purple 4mm
Loop Stitch

very dk yellow-green
floss
Stem Stitch

white floss
French Knot

dk yellow-green 4mm
Straight Stitch

Flower: Work a cone-shaped flower head with a few small loose Straight Stitches at the top, followed by larger Loop Stitches toward bottom. Lightly flatten each Loop Stitch and use white, cream, black, or flower-colored floss to anchor it with a French Knot. Stem-Stitch stems with floss.
Leaves: Work five Straight Stitches with all bases touching and the center stitch on top.
Flower colors: white, cream, salmon, pink, mauve, red, lavender, blue, purple, bi-color

Lavender (Lavandula)

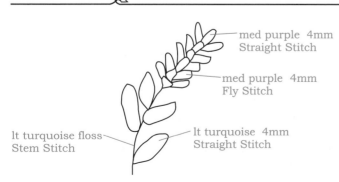

med purple 4mm
Straight Stitch

med purple 4mm
Fly Stitch

lt turquoise floss
Stem Stitch

lt turquoise 4mm
Straight Stitch

Flower: Work a small Straight Stitch at tip then work a column of Fly Stitches (2 or 4mm). Stem-Stitch stem with floss.
Leaves: Work Straight Stitches alternating along stem.
Flower colors: white, pink, lavender, purple

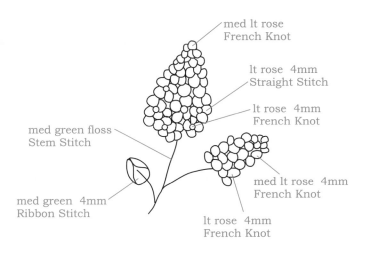

med lt rose
French Knot

lt rose 4mm
Straight Stitch

lt rose 4mm
French Knot

med green floss
Stem Stitch

med lt rose 4mm
French Knot

med green 4mm
Ribbon Stitch

lt rose 4mm
French Knot

Flower: We show two ways to stitch a lilac, depending upon the size of the flower head desired. For a large flower head, work short loose Straight Stitches to form four-petalled blossoms for the lower two-thirds; work a French Knot at center of some of the petalled blossoms. Work French Knots in a slightly darker color value for the upper third. Occasionally add extra Straight Stitches and French Knots to fill the cone equally with stitches. For a small flower head, stitch a slightly curved cone shape of French Knots, gradually increasing the size of the knots from tip to base; use a darker color value toward top of cone.

Leaves: Work a Ribbon Stitch (4 or 7mm). Stem-Stitch vein and stem with floss.

Flower colors: white, cream, pink, rose, violet, lavender, purple

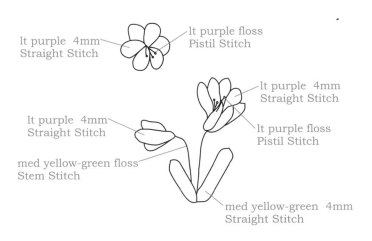

lt purple 4mm
Straight Stitch

lt purple floss
Pistil Stitch

lt purple 4mm
Straight Stitch

lt purple 4mm
Straight Stitch

lt purple floss
Pistil Stitch

med yellow-green floss
Stem Stitch

med yellow-green 4mm
Straight Stitch

Flower: Work two concentric circles of three petals each with Straight Stitches (4 or 7mm). There is no central open area when the inner circle of petals is formed. Work three to six Pistil Stitches with floss in the center of the flower. For a side view, work overlapping Straight Stitches with the middle stitch on top. Stem-Stitch the stem with floss.

Note: This form of blossom can be used for a Lily, Lily of the Nile, or Amaryllis.

Leaves: Work long Straight Stitches.

Flower colors: Lily—white, yellow, apricot, orange, copper, pink, rose, red; Lily of the Nile—white, blue; Amaryllis—white, salmon, pink, red

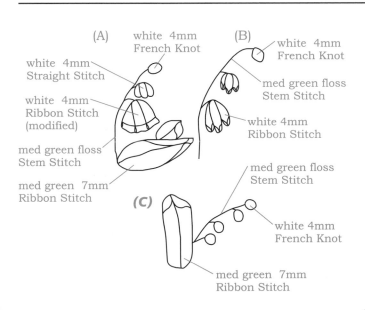

(A) white 4mm
French Knot

(B) white 4mm
French Knot

white 4mm
Straight Stitch

med green floss
Stem Stitch

white 4mm
Ribbon Stitch
(modified)

white 4mm
Ribbon Stitch

med green floss
Stem Stitch

med green floss
Stem Stitch

med green 7mm
Ribbon Stitch

(C)

white 4mm
French Knot

med green 7mm
Ribbon Stitch

Note: We show three ways to stitch these bell-like flowers. Stem-Stitch stems with floss.

Flower: Method A—Work a French Knot for a bud and three overlapping Straight Stitches for a partially opened flower. Work three modified Ribbon Stitches for a full flower, pulling the ribbon only until a "roll" appears at the end of the stitch. If pulled too tightly, the usual curves will appear at the end instead of the roll.

Method B—Work a French Knot for a bud. Work three overlapping Ribbon Stitches for partially opened buds.

Method C—Work French Knots, increasing their size toward base of stem.

Leaves: Work long Ribbon Stitches (or Straight Stitches). Use floss to Stem-Stitch vein.

Flower color: white, light pink

37

Lupine (Lupinus)

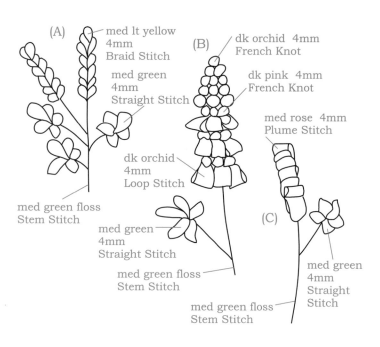

(A) med lt yellow 4mm Braid Stitch

med green 4mm Straight Stitch

(B) dk orchid 4mm French Knot

dk pink 4mm French Knot

med rose 4mm Plume Stitch

dk orchid 4mm Loop Stitch

med green floss Stem Stitch

med green 4mm Straight Stitch

(C)

med green 4mm Straight Stitch

med green floss Stem Stitch

med green floss Stem Stitch

Note: We show three ways to stitch these flower heads. Stem-Stitch all stems with floss.

Flower: Method A—Work flower head using Braid Stitch.

Method B—Work a cone-shaped flower head with French Knots of increasing size from tip for top third of shape. On the middle portion of the shape, alternate French Knots with rows of Loop Stitches; these French Knots can be a lighter color value with the Loop Stitches matching the topmost French Knots. In the lower area add a small Loop Stitch before stitching the French Knot (loop in one color and a lighter color for the knot).

Method C—Work flower head using Plume Stitch.

Leaves: Work five Straight Stitches (2 or 4mm) radiating from tip of stem.

Flower colors: white, cream, yellow, salmon, orange, pink, mauve, rose, red, lavender, blue, purple, bi-colors

Magnolia (Magnolia)

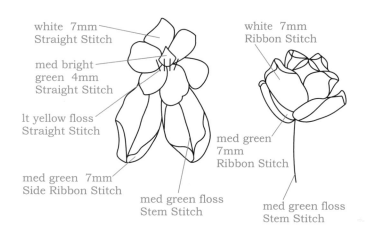

white 7mm Straight Stitch

med bright green 4mm Straight Stitch

lt yellow floss Straight Stitch

med green 7mm Side Ribbon Stitch

med green floss Stem Stitch

white 7mm Ribbon Stitch

med green 7mm Ribbon Stitch

med green floss Stem Stitch

Flower: Work six large, loose Straight Stitches (4 or 7mm), leaving a small central open area. At center, work one short Straight Stitch. Use floss to make short Straight Stitches at base. For a side view, work four or five overlapping Ribbon Stitches.

Leaves: Work two parallel Side Ribbon Stitches (4 or 7mm) with tips sharing the same point beneath petals. A small tacking stitch may be needed to keep ribbon edges from curling inward. Stem-Stitch vein (to hold ribbons together) and also the stem.

Flower colors: white, cream, yellow-green, pink, red-purple

Marigold (Tagetes)

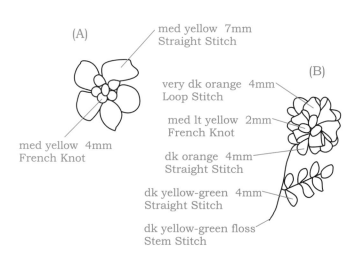

(A) med yellow 7mm Straight Stitch

(B)

very dk orange 4mm Loop Stitch

med lt yellow 2mm French Knot

dk orange 4mm Straight Stitch

med yellow 4mm French Knot

dk yellow-green 4mm Straight Stitch

dk yellow-green floss Stem Stitch

Note: We show two methods to stitch marigold blossoms.

Flower: Method A—Work a circle of five loose Straight Stitches (4 or 7mm), leaving a central open area. Fill open area with loose French Knots (2 or 4mm).

Method B—Work outer circle of 10 or more Straight Stitches around an open area. Work an inner circle of Loop Stitches. Work French Knots at center.

Leaves: Stem-Stitch stems with floss. Work seven or eight Straight Stitches alternating along stem and at tip.

Flower colors: white, bright yellow, bright orange, burnt orange, gold, russet-red

Berries: Work loose French Knots (2 or 4mm). Usually there are three to seven berries per cluster.
Leaves: Work Ribbon Stitches (4 or 7mm). Work a long Straight Stitch with floss for vein when using the wider ribbon. Use floss to work a thick stem with Stem Stitch.
Berry colors: creamy white

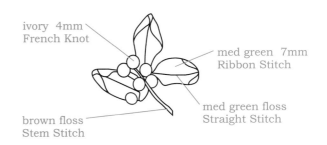

ivory 4mm
French Knot

med green 7mm
Ribbon Stitch

med green floss
Straight Stitch

brown floss
Stem Stitch

Note: We show three methods to stitch narcissus blossoms.
Flower: Method A—For a large full-face flower, work two concentric circles of three loose Straight Stitches, leaving a small central open area. At center, work a short Loop Stitch, then anchor it with a French Knot.
Method B—For side view of the flower, work three petals with loose Straight Stitches (4 or 7mm); add a small Loop Stitch where petals meet.
Method C—For a small full-face flower, stitch two concentric circles of three short loose Straight Stitches, leaving small central open area. In open area stitch a loose two-wrap French Knot.
Leaves: Work long Straight, Twisted Straight or Ribbon Stitches.
Flower colors: outer petals—white, cream, yellow; center petals—white, cream, light and bright yellow, apricot, orange

(A)

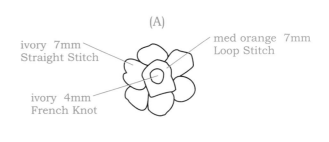

ivory 7mm
Straight Stitch

med orange 7mm
Loop Stitch

ivory 4mm
French Knot

(B)

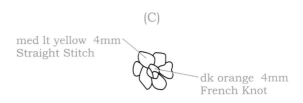

med orange 4mm
Loop Stitch

ivory 7mm
Straight Stitch

(C)

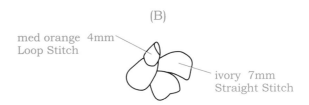

med lt yellow 4mm
Straight Stitch

dk orange 4mm
French Knot

Flower: Work five loose Straight Stitches (4 or 7mm) radiating from a small open area. Use floss to tightly couch each Straight Stitch twice near the base. Use floss to fill central open area with French Knots.
Leaves: Work two Side Ribbon Stitches (4 or 7mm) next to each other so bases and tips meet to make a round leaf; leaf edges may need to be tacked with matching floss to retain the shape. Use floss to Stem-Stitch stems and veins.
Flower colors: cream, light and bright yellow, apricot, orange, red, maroon

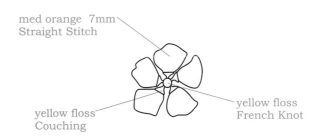

med orange 7mm
Straight Stitch

yellow floss
Couching

yellow floss
French Knot

Orchid (Cymbidium, Cyperipedium, Cattleya)

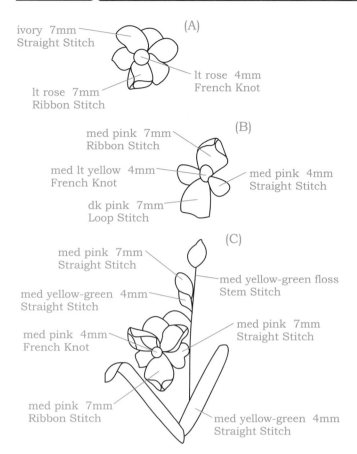

ivory 7mm
Straight Stitch

(A)

lt rose 4mm
French Knot

lt rose 7mm
Ribbon Stitch

med pink 7mm
Ribbon Stitch

(B)

med lt yellow 4mm
French Knot

med pink 4mm
Straight Stitch

dk pink 7mm
Loop Stitch

(C)

med pink 7mm
Straight Stitch

med yellow-green floss
Stem Stitch

med yellow-green 4mm
Straight Stitch

med pink 4mm
French Knot

med pink 7mm
Straight Stitch

med pink 7mm
Ribbon Stitch

med yellow-green 4mm
Straight Stitch

Note: We show three methods to work orchid blossoms.

Flower: Method A *(Cymbidium)*—Work three Straight Stitches (4 or 7mm) radiating from a central point. On top of and alternating with these three stitches, work two more Straight Stitches. Work one Ribbon Stitch at bottom to fill circle. Work a French Knot (2 or 4mm) at center.

Method B *(Cyperipedium)*—For this version, often called lady slipper, work petals (4 or 7mm) with different stitches radiating from a central point. At the top, work a large Ribbon Stitch; work a small Straight Stitch on each side and one Loop Stitch at bottom. Work a French Knot at center.

Method C *(Cattleya)*—Work three Straight Stitches (4 or 7mm) radiating from a central point. On top of and alternating with these three stitches, work three slightly longer Ribbon Stitches (4 or 7mm). Work a French Knot (2 or 4mm) at center.

Bud: Work a Straight Stitch (4 or 7mm). Work a Straight Stitch (4 or 7mm) for calyx.

Leaves: Work a Straight Stitch. If a bent leaf is desired, use matching floss to tack in position.

Flower colors: *Cymbidium*—white, yellow, green, bronze, pink, most with yellow throat; *Cyperipedium*—white, yellow, rose, yellow-green, purple-brown, bi-color; *Cattleya*—white, yellow, red-orange, green, bronze, lavender, purple

Pansy (Viola)

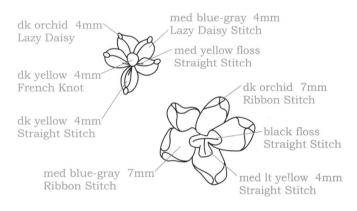

dk orchid 4mm
Lazy Daisy

med blue-gray 4mm
Lazy Daisy Stitch

med yellow floss
Straight Stitch

dk yellow 4mm
French Knot

dk orchid 7mm
Ribbon Stitch

dk yellow 4mm
Straight Stitch

black floss
Straight Stitch

med blue-gray 7mm
Ribbon Stitch

med lt yellow 4mm
Straight Stitch

Flower: For a small pansy work five Lazy Daisy Stitches radiating from a small central open area. Work a short Straight Stitch on lower petal and a French Knot at center. Using floss, work Straight Stitches on three lower petals.

For a larger pansy, work five Ribbon Stitches radiating from a small central open area. Work Straight Stitches over the three bottom petals. Use floss to work a Straight Stitch over each bottom petal.

Leaves: Stem-Stitch each stem with floss. Work three Straight Stitches (4 or 7mm) at end of each stem.

Flower colors: white, yellow, apricot, rose, maroon, blue, lavender, violet, purple, bi-color

Peony (Paeonia)

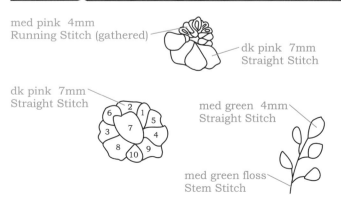

med pink 4mm
Running Stitch (gathered)

dk pink 7mm
Straight Stitch

dk pink 7mm
Straight Stitch

med green 4mm
Straight Stitch

med green floss
Stem Stitch

Flower: For the full blossom, work ten Straight Stitches (4 or 7mm) following the numerical sequence. For the side view of a special variety, work four Straight Stitches for petals across lower half. For the top half, cut a 2" piece of ribbon; using matching floss, work Running Stitch along one long edge of the ribbon; pull to gather into a tight circle. Turn under raw ends and tack to fabric.

Leaves: Stem-Stitch stems with floss. Work three to five Straight Stitches (4 or 7mm) which meet along stem with one at the tip.

Flower colors: white, cream, pink, rose, red

Flower: Work five loose Straight Stitches (4 or 7mm) around a small central open area. Work a French Knot (floss or 2mm) at center. Use floss to Stem-Stitch the stem. The flowers usually occur in the notches between the leaf stem and the vine stem.

Bud: Work a Ribbon Stitch (4 or 7mm) in flower color.

Leaves: Work Straight Stitches (4 or 7mm) at tip of stem and opposite each other along the curving vine.

Flower colors: white, pink, rose, light or dark lilac-blue

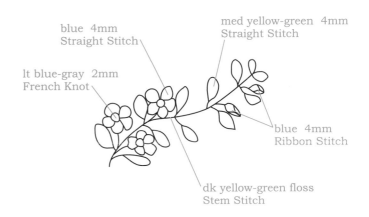

blue 4mm
Straight Stitch

med yellow-green 4mm
Straight Stitch

lt blue-gray 2mm
French Knot

blue 4mm
Ribbon Stitch

dk yellow-green floss
Stem Stitch

Pine Cone: Work Cretan Stitch in a triangular shape. Begin at top of shape and use normal tension for the stitches; work lower portion with increasingly looser stitches.

Pine Needles: Work Straight Stitches (floss or 2mm ribbon) near base of cone.

bronze 4mm
Cretan Stitch

dk yellow-green 2mm
Straight Stitch

med yellow-green 4mm
Straight Stitch

Flower: Work two concentric circles of modified Lazy Daisy Stitches (4 or 7mm). Work five bracts for the lowest circles, each bract radiating from a central open area. Work second circle of five bracts on top of and between bracts of the first circle. For the modified stitches, only the loops of the Lazy Daisy Stitches are formed with ribbon; use matching floss to make the tack-down portion of each stitch. Fill center open area with French Knots.

Leaves: Work long Straight or Lazy Daisy Stitches (4 or 7mm), between and underneath bracts.

Flower colors: white, pink, salmon, red, bi-color

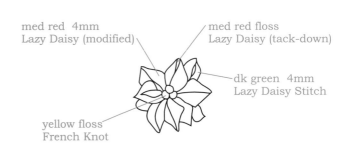

med red 4mm
Lazy Daisy (modified)

med red floss
Lazy Daisy (tack-down)

dk green 4mm
Lazy Daisy Stitch

yellow floss
French Knot

Poppy *(Eschscholzia, Papaver)*

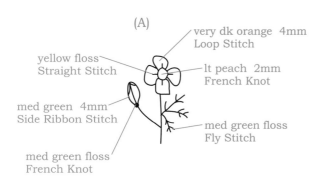

(A)

yellow floss
Straight Stitch

very dk orange 4mm
Loop Stitch

lt peach 2mm
French Knot

med green 4mm
Side Ribbon Stitch

med green floss
Fly Stitch

med green floss
French Knot

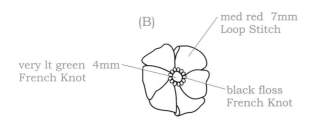

(B)

med red 7mm
Loop Stitch

very lt green 4mm
French Knot

black floss
French Knot

Flower: For California poppy (*Eschscholzia*) flower (A), work four Loop Stitches (4 or 7mm) around a small central open area. Use floss to make a Straight Stitch at base of each Loop Stitch. Work a French Knot (2 or 4mm) at center .

For Oriental or Iceland poppy (*Papaver*) flower (B), work four to six Loop Stitches (4 or 7mm) around a central open area. Work a French Knot at center of open area. Use black floss to surround the green knot with French Knots.

Bud: California poppy—Work two Side Ribbon Stitches (4 or 7mm) with tips meeting at a single point. Use floss to work a French Knot at base of bud.

Leaves: California poppy—Use floss to Stem-Stitch stem. Work Fly Stitches (floss or 2mm) at stem ends.

Flower colors: California—ivory, yellow, bright orange, red-orange, pink, rose; Oriental—white, salmon, red-orange, rose, red; Iceland—white, ivory, yellow, apricot, salmon, orange, pink, rose, red

Primrose *(Primula)*

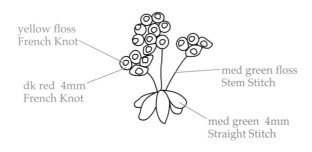

yellow floss
French Knot

dk red 4mm
French Knot

med green floss
Stem Stitch

med green 4mm
Straight Stitch

Flower: Work three to seven loose French Knots with ribbon. Use floss to work a French Knot on top of each ribbon knot. Use a combination of 7mm with 4mm ribbon or 4mm ribbon with floss. Use floss to Stem-Stitch stems.

Leaves: Work Straight Stitches (4 or 7mm) at base of stems.

Flower colors: white, cream, yellow, apricot, pink, rose, red, blue, purple—all with yellow centers

Pussywillow *(Salix)*

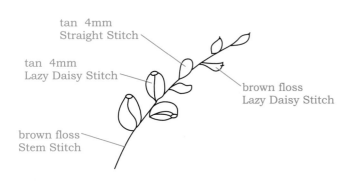

tan 4mm
Straight Stitch

tan 4mm
Lazy Daisy Stitch

brown floss
Lazy Daisy Stitch

brown floss
Stem Stitch

Catkins: Use floss to Stem-Stitch stem. Work short Straight Stitches or Lazy Daisy Stitches alternating on stem.

Catkin colors: cream, warm gray, pink, taupe

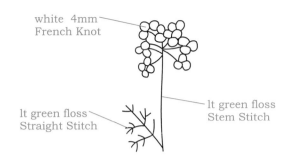

white 4mm
French Knot

lt green floss
Stem Stitch

lt green floss
Straight Stitch

Flower: Stem-Stitch stem and rays with floss. Four or five long rays radiate from tip of flower stem, alternating with three or four short rays. At end of each ray, work two to four small French Knots (floss, 2 or 4mm).
Leaves: Use floss to Straight-Stitch a finely divided leaf.
Flower colors: white, cream, pink

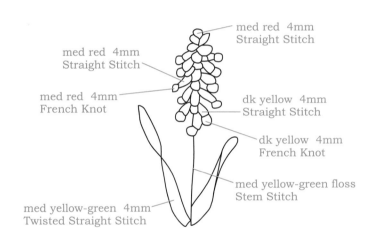

med red 4mm
Straight Stitch

med red 4mm
Straight Stitch

med red 4mm
French Knot

dk yellow 4mm
Straight Stitch

dk yellow 4mm
French Knot

med yellow-green floss
Stem Stitch

med yellow-green 4mm
Twisted Straight Stitch

Flower: Work three to five short Straight Stitches at tip of flower head. Continuing down the flower head, make longer Straight Stitches with a French Knot at each outer tip. Change color, if desired, for bottom group of stitches.
Leaves: Work long Twisted Straight Stitches. If a bent leaf is desired, use matching floss to tack in position.
Flower colors: bi-color heads from tip to base—red to green, green to yellow, medium orange to light orange, light orange to yellow, medium green to light green

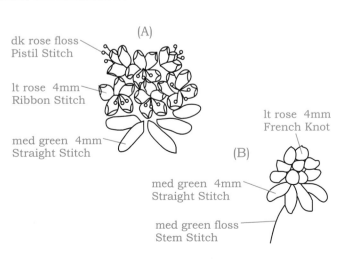

(A)

dk rose floss
Pistil Stitch

lt rose 4mm
Ribbon Stitch

med green 4mm
Straight Stitch

lt rose 4mm
French Knot

(B)

med green 4mm
Straight Stitch

med green floss
Stem Stitch

Flower: For a large flower head (A), work groups of five Ribbon Stitches (4 or 7mm) radiating from a central point; for a side view of a flowerette, work three Ribbon Stitches. At center of each flowerette, use floss to work three to six Pistil Stitches. Group flowers in an open semicircle.
For small flower heads (B), work seven to ten loose double-wrap French Knots in an open semi-circle.
Leaves: Work three to five Straight Stitches (4 or 7mm) directly beneath flower cluster. Use floss to Stem-Stitch stem.
Flower colors: white, cream, yellow, apricot, salmon, pink, rose, red

43

ROSES

Bradford Rose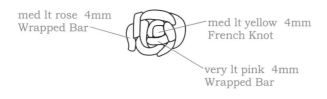

Note: There are many ways to stitch roses and rosebuds. Rather than duplicating specific varieties, these generic roses are named by the type of embroidery stitch used to make them. They may be worked in your choice of colors.

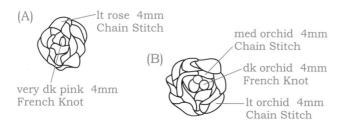

med lt rose 4mm Wrapped Bar

med lt yellow 4mm French Knot

very lt pink 4mm Wrapped Bar

Work a loose French Knot at center. Working in a clockwise direction, make three curved Wrapped Bars (4 or 7mm) of equal length surrounding center knot. Use another color value to work four or five curved Wrapped Bars encircling first group of bars. Shading can occur with either the lighter value or darker value surrounding center.

Chain Stitch Rose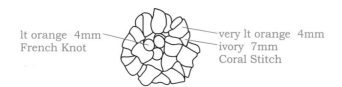

(A) lt rose 4mm Chain Stitch

very dk pink 4mm French Knot

(B)

med orchid 4mm Chain Stitch

dk orchid 4mm French Knot

lt orchid 4mm Chain Stitch

For a bi-color rose (A), make a French Knot at center. Use a lighter color value to work two rows of Chain Stitches around knot. For a tri-color rose (B), choose light, medium, and dark values of a color. Work three French Knots at center with dark value. Surround the knots with one row of Chain Stitch with medium value and an outer row of Chain Stitch with lightest value.

Coral Stitch Rose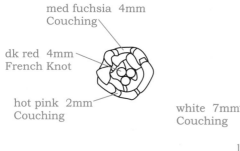

lt orange 4mm French Knot

very lt orange 4mm ivory 7mm Coral Stitch

Work three loose French Knots at center with a dark color value. Place a 4mm ribbon, centered, on top of a 7mm ribbon and treat the two layers as one; work two rows of Coral Stitch around central knots.

Couched Rose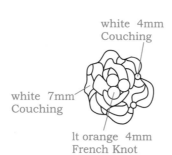

med fuchsia 4mm Couching

dk red 4mm French Knot

hot pink 2mm Couching

white 4mm Couching

white 7mm Couching

lt orange 4mm French Knot

Work three French Knots at center of rose. Surround the knots by couching one ribbon with another in a circular clockwise manner; use contrasting or matching ribbons for the couching. For a medium size rose, use 2mm ribbon to couch 4mm ribbon. For a large rose, use 4mm ribbon to couch 7mm ribbon.

Crossed Chain Rose

Work this rose with the same sequence and color shading as for the Chain Stitch Rose on (page 44), substituting Crossed Chain Stitches for the Chain Stitches.

med red 4mm
Crossed Chain Stitch

dk red 4mm
French Knot

Fishbone Stitch Rose

Work Fishbone Stitch following the numerical sequence, always working from outside edge toward center. Work an occasional Straight Stitch in a darker color value between the previously worked stitches. Add Straight Stitches at base of rose.

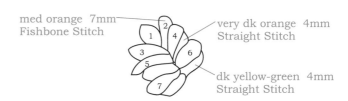

med orange 7mm
Fishbone Stitch

very dk orange 4mm
Straight Stitch

dk yellow-green 4mm
Straight Stitch

Folded Ribbon Rose

Work Folded Ribbon Stitch, page 11, in desired color. Vary the length of the ribbon to change size of rose.

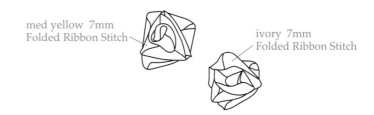

med yellow 7mm
Folded Ribbon Stitch

ivory 7mm
Folded Ribbon Stitch

Gathered Rose

Thread a needle with floss to match ribbon and set aside. Cut ribbon (4 or 7mm) into a 6" length. *Note:* You can vary the size of the rose by cutting a longer (A) or shorter (C) piece of ribbon. Fold one end under and use matching floss color to work Running Stitches very close to one long edge for an inch or so. Gather with folded end under and tack to background fabric with floss. Gather another inch or so of ribbon and spiral it around the previously tacked ribbon. Continue in this manner until all ribbon is gathered and tacked in a shape resembling a full rose. Bring raw end under the last gathered spiral and tack so end is hidden. To form a bi-colored rose (B), place a 4mm ribbon on top of a 7mm ribbon, aligning edges along one long edge. Sew ribbons together with Running Stitch in floss and then proceed to gather ribbon as described above.

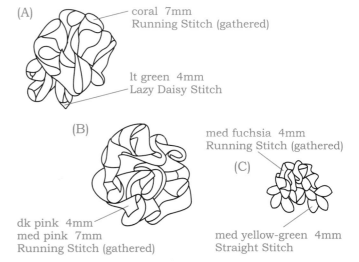

(A)

coral 7mm
Running Stitch (gathered)

lt green 4mm
Lazy Daisy Stitch

(B)

med fuchsia 4mm
Running Stitch (gathered)

(C)

dk pink 4mm
med pink 7mm
Running Stitch (gathered)

med yellow-green 4mm
Straight Stitch

ROSES
Loop Stitch Rose

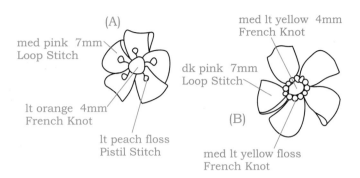

med pink 7mm
Loop Stitch

(A)

lt orange 4mm
French Knot

lt peach floss
Pistil Stitch

med lt yellow 4mm
French Knot

dk pink 7mm
Loop Stitch

(B)

med lt yellow floss
French Knot

Work five Loop Stitches (4 or 7mm) around a central opening. The length of the loop is determined by width of ribbon and effect desired. For (A), use floss to work one to three Pistil Stitches at base of each petal. Work a loose French Knot at center. For (B), work Loop Stitch petals in same manner; work a French Knot at center and surround it with French Knots worked with floss.

Pin Rose

(A)

(B)

very lt orange 4mm
Winding Technique

dk orange 4mm
French Knot

Using a long straight pin, take an ⅛" bite into background fabric. Bring ribbon-threaded needle (2, 4 or 7mm) up through fabric next to pin; wind ribbon around pin (A) until desired size is reached. Using a single strand of floss to match rose, tack down opposite sides of coil. Remove pin. Work a loose French Knot (2 or 4mm) in a darker color value at center (B).

Ribbon Stitch Rose

very dk fuchsia
7mm
Ribbon Stitch

med lt yellow 4mm
French Knot

med lt yellow floss
Pistil Stitch

Work five Ribbon Stitches (4 or 7mm) radiating from a small central open area. Using floss, add one to three Pistil Stitches at base of each petal. Work a loose French Knot at center.

Scroll Stitch Rose

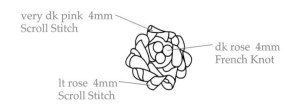

very dk pink 4mm
Scroll Stitch

dk rose 4mm
French Knot

lt rose 4mm
Scroll Stitch

Choose three color values (light, medium, dark) of ribbon. Use dark value to work three loose French Knots at center. Work two concentric circles of Scroll Stitches in the medium value around knots. Use light value to work one semicircular row of Scroll Stitches around lower half of rose.

Work eight Side Ribbon Stitches (4 or 7mm) following the numerical sequence on the enlarged version. Make petals one, two, seven, and eight shorter than the others. Work petals nine and ten in the center of the flower, covering the center; work petal eleven over and between petals nine and ten.

very lt pink 7mm
Side Ribbon Stitch

Spider Web Rose

Use floss to work the base legs of a Spider Web; the color will not show. Choose three color values of ribbon for weaving. Weave around inner portion of base with medium value and finish outer portion with light value. Use dark value to work a French Knot at center.

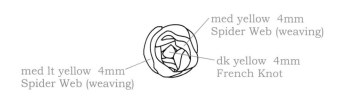

med yellow 4mm
Spider Web (weaving)

dk yellow 4mm
French Knot

med lt yellow 4mm
Spider Web (weaving)

Stem Stitch Rose

Work a loose French Knot at center. Work concentric circles of short, loose Stem Stitches in a clockwise direction around knot.

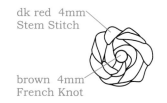

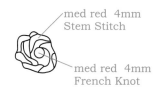

dk red 4mm
Stem Stitch

brown 4mm
French Knot

med red 4mm
Stem Stitch

med red 4mm
French Knot

Straight Stitch Rose

Work five loose Straight Stitches (4 or 7mm) radiating from a small central open area. Use floss to work one, two, or three Pistil Stitches at base of each petal. Work a loose French Knot at center.

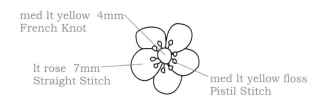

med lt yellow 4mm
French Knot

lt rose 7mm
Straight Stitch

med lt yellow floss
Pistil Stitch

ROSES
Wrapped Bar Rose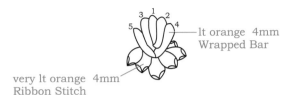

3 1 2
5   4

lt orange 4mm
Wrapped Bar

very lt orange 4mm
Ribbon Stitch

Work five Wrapped Bars following numerical sequence; place the last two below the base of the first three. Work five or six Ribbon Stitches encircling bottom third of partially formed flower.

ROSEBUDS
Bi-Color Rosebud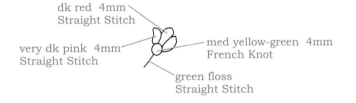

dk red 4mm
Straight Stitch

very dk pink 4mm
Straight Stitch

med yellow-green 4mm
French Knot

green floss
Straight Stitch

Work a Straight Stitch in a dark color value. Use a lighter color value to work a Straight Stitch slightly below and on each side of first stitch. Work a French Knot at base of bud. Use floss to Straight-Stitch the stem.

Decorative Lazy Daisy Rosebud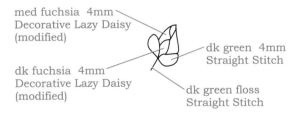

med fuchsia 4mm
Decorative Lazy Daisy
(modified)

dk fuchsia 4mm
Decorative Lazy Daisy
(modified)

dk green 4mm
Straight Stitch

dk green floss
Straight Stitch

Work a modified Decorative Lazy Daisy Stitch. Use a medium color value for the Lazy Daisy portion and a dark color value for the center stitch. Work Straight Stitches for leaves. Use floss to Straight-Stitch the stem.

🌸 Detached Twisted Chain Rosebud

Work a Detached Twisted Chain Stitch (4 or 7mm) for the bud. Work two Straight Stitches (4 or 7mm) overlapping the base of bud for leaves. Use floss to Straight-Stitch the stem.

med yellow-green 4mm
Straight Stitch

lt orange 4mm
Detached Twisted Chain

med yellow-green floss
Straight Stitch

🌸 French Knot Rosebud

Work a very loose two-wrap French Knot (4 or 7mm). The ribbon width determines the size of the bud.

med pink 4mm
French Knot

med pink 7mm
French Knot

🌸 Lazy Daisy Rosebud

Work a Lazy Daisy Stitch (4 or 7mm) for the bud. Work an Extended Fly Stitch for leaves.

med yellow 4mm
Lazy Daisy

dk yellow-green 4mm
Extended Fly Stitch

🌸 Lazy Daisy/French Knot Rosebud

Work a Lazy Daisy Stitch. Work a French Knot of a different color in center of Lazy Daisy Stitch. Work an Extended Fly Stitch at base of bud.

med red 4mm
Lazy Daisy

med yellow-green 2mm
Extended Fly Stitch

dk orange 4mm
French Knot

ROSEBUDS
Padded Straight Stitch Rosebud

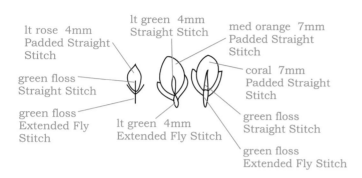

lt rose 4mm
Padded Straight
Stitch

lt green 4mm
Straight Stitch

med orange 7mm
Padded Straight
Stitch

coral 7mm
Padded Straight
Stitch

green floss
Straight Stitch

green floss
Extended Fly
Stitch

lt green 4mm
Extended Fly Stitch

green floss
Straight Stitch

green floss
Extended Fly Stitch

Work a Padded Straight Stitch (4 or 7mm) in desired color. Use floss or ribbon to work one vertical Stem Stitch at base of bud and an Extended Fly Stitch below bud.

Ribbon Stitch/French Knot Rosebud

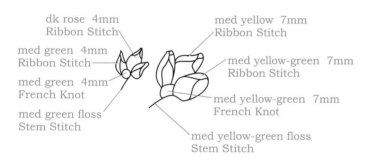

dk rose 4mm
Ribbon Stitch

med yellow 7mm
Ribbon Stitch

med green 4mm
Ribbon Stitch

med green 4mm
French Knot

med green floss
Stem Stitch

med yellow-green 7mm
Ribbon Stitch

med yellow-green 7mm
French Knot

med yellow-green floss
Stem Stitch

Work a Ribbon Stitch (4 or 7mm) in desired flower color. Work two Ribbon Stitches (4 or 7mm) and a French Knot at base of bud. Use floss to Stem-Stitch stem.

Side Ribbon Stitch Rosebud

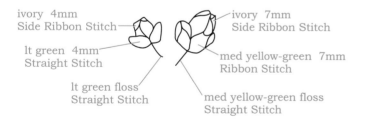

ivory 4mm
Side Ribbon Stitch

lt green 4mm
Straight Stitch

lt green floss
Straight Stitch

ivory 7mm
Side Ribbon Stitch

med yellow-green 7mm
Ribbon Stitch

med yellow-green floss
Straight Stitch

Work two Side Ribbon Stitches (4 or 7mm) with their tips and bases touching. Work two Ribbon Stitches or Straight Stitches (4 or 7mm) at base of bud for leaves. Use floss to Straight-Stitch stem.

Straight Stitch Rosebud

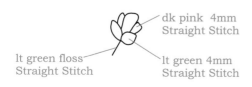

dk pink 4mm
Straight Stitch

lt green floss
Straight Stitch

lt green 4mm
Straight Stitch

Work three Straight Stitches (4 or 7mm) so their bases meet. Stitch two Straight Stitches (4 or 7mm) to cover base of bud. Use floss to Straight-Stitch stem.

Work a loose Straight Stitch (4 or 7mm) in desired flower color. Work a French Knot (2 or 4mm) in a darker color value over tip of Straight Stitch. Work Straight Stitches at base of bud for leaves. Use floss to Straight-Stitch stem.

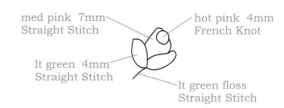

med pink 7mm
Straight Stitch

hot pink 4mm
French Knot

lt green 4mm
Straight Stitch

lt green floss
Straight Stitch

🌸 Rose Bush

Use floss to Stem-Stitch branches and stems and to work leaves in Lazy Daisy Stitches. Work Folded Ribbon Stitch for each rose blossom.

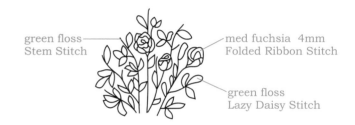

green floss
Stem Stitch

med fuchsia 4mm
Folded Ribbon Stitch

green floss
Lazy Daisy Stitch

🌸 Rose Leaves

Work Straight Stitches, Ribbon Stitches, or Lazy Daisy Stitches (4 or 7mm) for leaves. Use matching floss to Stem-Stitch stems.

med green 4mm
Ribbon Stitch

med green 4mm
Straight Stitch

med green 4mm
Straight Stitch

med green floss
Stem Stitch

med green floss
Stem Stitch

med yellow-green 7mm
Straight Stitch

med yellow-green 7mm
Lazy Daisy Stitch

med yellow-green floss
Stem Stitch

med green 7mm
Ribbon Stitch

med green 7mm
Ribbon Stitch

med green floss
Stem Stitch

Salvia *(Salvia)*

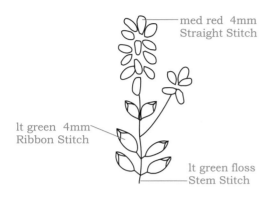

med red 4mm
Straight Stitch

lt green 4mm
Ribbon Stitch

lt green floss
Stem Stitch

Flower: Work Straight Stitches in loose whorl arrangements. Use floss to Stem-Stitch stems.
Leaves: Work pairs of Ribbon Stitches (4 or 7mm) opposite each other at ends of short leaf stems.
Flower colors: white, cream, salmon, pink, rose, red, lilac, blue, purple

Scilla *(Scilla)*

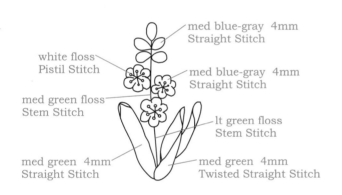

med blue-gray 4mm
Straight Stitch

white floss
Pistil Stitch

med blue-gray 4mm
Straight Stitch

med green floss
Stem Stitch

lt green floss
Stem Stitch

med green 4mm
Straight Stitch

med green 4mm
Twisted Straight Stitch

Flower: Use floss to Stem-Stitch stem. Work six Straight Stitches around a central point. Use floss to work a Pistil Stitch at base of each petal.
Bud: Work Straight Stitches.
Leaves: Work long, loose Twisted Straight Stitches or Straight Stitches (4 or 7mm).
Flower colors: white, pink, blue

Snapdragon *(Antirrhinum)*

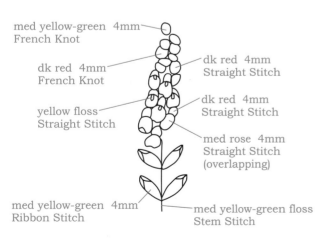

med yellow-green 4mm
French Knot

dk red 4mm
French Knot

dk red 4mm
Straight Stitch

yellow floss
Straight Stitch

dk red 4mm
Straight Stitch

med rose 4mm
Straight Stitch
(overlapping)

med yellow-green 4mm
Ribbon Stitch

med yellow-green floss
Stem Stitch

Bud: Begin at tip of flower head and work French Knots: green, then dark flower color. For remaining buds, work Straight Stitches in dark flower color.
Flower: For top half of bi-color blossom, work a short Straight Stitch (4 or 7mm) with a dark color value; work an overlapping Straight Stitch with a lighter value for lower half of blossom. Arrange flowers in loose whorls. On some blossoms, use floss to work a loose Straight Stitch at center.
Leaves: Use floss to Stem-Stitch stem. Work Ribbon Stitches opposite each other along stem.
Flower colors: white, cream, yellow, orange, rose, scarlet, purple, bi-color

Note: We show two snowdrop varieties. Use floss to Stem-Stitch stems.
Flower: Eranthis (A)—Work three Straight Stitches (4 or 7mm) with a short middle stitch and overlapping side stitches. Use floss to work a French Knot at base of petals and two adjacent Straight Stitches at tip of center petal. *Leucojum* (B)—Work three Straight Stitches (4 or 7mm) with two short side stitches and a long overlapping middle stitch. Work two adjacent Straight Stitches at tip of each petal.
Leaves: Work long Straight Stitches (4mm or floss).
Flower color: white with green

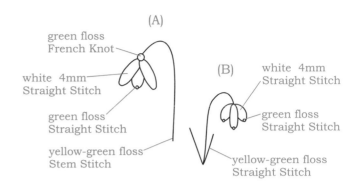

(A)
green floss
French Knot
white 4mm
Straight Stitch
green floss
Straight Stitch
yellow-green floss
Stem Stitch

(B)
white 4mm
Straight Stitch
green floss
Straight Stitch
yellow-green floss
Straight Stitch

Flower: Work 12-16 Straight Stitches (2, 4 or 7mm) around a large central open area. Work a cluster of light brown French Knots (floss, 2 or 4mm), surrounded by a ring of medium brown French Knots (floss, 2 or 4mm) at center.
Leaves: Work two Side Ribbon Stitches (4 or 7mm) with their tips touching. Use floss to Stem-Stitch stems and vein.
Flower colors: yellow, orange, red-brown, mahogany

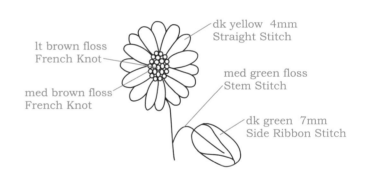

lt brown floss
French Knot
med brown floss
French Knot
dk yellow 4mm
Straight Stitch
med green floss
Stem Stitch
dk green 7mm
Side Ribbon Stitch

Flower: For a full blossom (A), work four Straight Stitches and one Ribbon Stitch (4 or 7mm) with folded edges of Ribbon Stitch at center. For a side view (B), work three Straight Stitches (4 or 7mm) with their bases sharing a single point. For the calyx, work two short Straight Stitches overlapping base of petals.
Leaves: Work pairs of Straight Stitches (4 or 7mm) opposite each other. Use floss to Stem-Stitch stems and tendrils.
Flower colors: white, cream, apricot, pink, rose, red, blue, lavender, purple

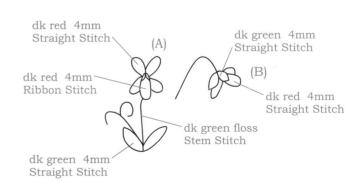

dk red 4mm
Straight Stitch
(A)
dk red 4mm
Ribbon Stitch
dk green 4mm
Straight Stitch

dk green 4mm
Straight Stitch
(B)
dk red 4mm
Straight Stitch
dk green floss
Stem Stitch

Trillium 🌸 *(Trillium)*

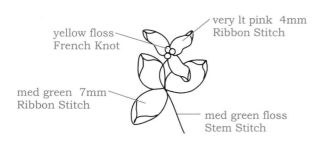

yellow floss
French Knot

very lt pink 4mm
Ribbon Stitch

med green 7mm
Ribbon Stitch

med green floss
Stem Stitch

Note: Stitch leaves and stem before working flower at end of stem that emerges from a cluster of three leaves.
Leaves: Work three Ribbon Stitches with bases sharing a central point. Use floss to Stem-Stitch stem.
Flower: Work three Ribbon Stitches (4 or 7mm) radiating from a small center open area. Using floss work three to five small French Knots (floss or 4mm) at center.
Flower colors: white, cream, yellow, pink, pink-brown, cerise

Tulips 🌷 *(Tulipa)*

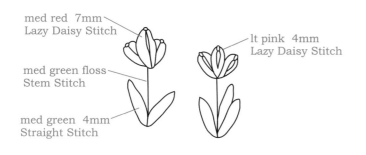

med red 7mm
Lazy Daisy Stitch

lt pink 4mm
Lazy Daisy Stitch

med green floss
Stem Stitch

med green 4mm
Straight Stitch

Flower: Work three Lazy Daisy Stitches (4 or 7mm) with the middle petal on top of and slightly longer than the side petals. Use floss to Stem-Stitch the stems.
Leaves: Work long Straight Stitches (4 or 7mm).
Flower colors: white, cream, yellow, orange, pink, rose, red, lavender, purple, bi-color

Violet 🌸 *(Viola)*

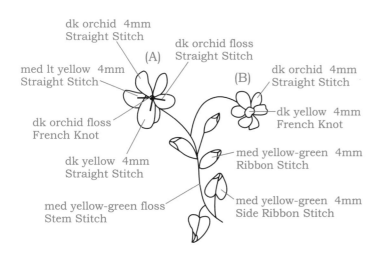

dk orchid 4mm
Straight Stitch

dk orchid floss
Straight Stitch

(A)

(B)

dk orchid 4mm
Straight Stitch

med lt yellow 4mm
Straight Stitch

dk yellow 4mm
French Knot

dk orchid floss
French Knot

dk yellow 4mm
Straight Stitch

med yellow-green 4mm
Ribbon Stitch

med yellow-green floss
Stem Stitch

med yellow-green 4mm
Side Ribbon Stitch

Note: We show two kinds of violets and two kinds of leaves, all on the same stem. Use floss to Stem-Stitch the stems.
Flower: For a bi-color flower (A), choose three color values for the short, loose Straight Stitches. Work the top two in a dark color value, the middle two in a light color value, and the bottom two in a medium color value, overlapping each other. Use floss to work a French Knot and three Straight Stitches at center. For a single color flower (B), work six short, loose Straight Stitches, all with the same color value. Work a French Knot at center.
Leaves: For oval leaves, work Ribbon stitches. For heart-shaped leaves, work two Side Ribbon Stitches with their tips touching and bases apart.
Flower colors: white, yellow, blue, lavender, violet, purple, bi-color (purple and yellow)

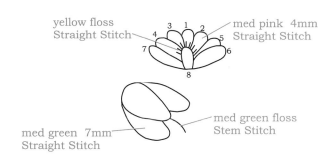

Flower: Work eight Straight Stitches (4 or 7mm) following numerical sequence. Use floss to work Straight Stitches above petal #8.

Leaves: Work two or three Straight Stitches (4 or 7mm) with their tips touching. When making three Straight Stitches, work the middle one last to overlap the side stitches. Use floss to Stem-Stitch stem.

Flower colors: white, cream, yellow, copper, pink, red

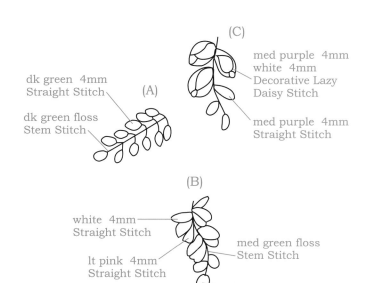

Note: We show two ways (Methods B and C) to stitch these cascading flower stems. Use floss to Stem-Stitch all stems.

Flower: Method B—Work pairs of Straight Stitches downward along the stem, tapering to single stitches at tip. Occasionally work a Straight Stitch in a contrasting color on the upper half of the cascade. Method C—work Decorative Lazy Daisy Stitches for upper half of cascade; use a contrasting color for the center filling stitch. Work Straight Stitches toward tip.

Leaves: (A) Work short Straight Stitches (4 or 7mm) opposite each other along stem.

Flower colors: white, pink, mauve, violet, blue, lavender, purple

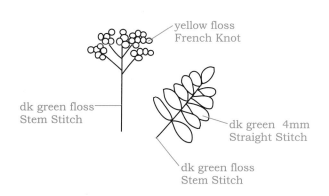

Flower: Use floss to Stem-Stitch stem. Work a slightly flattened flower head of French Knots (floss, 2 or 4mm) at tips of stems.

Leaves: Work Straight Stitches alternating along stem.

Flower colors: white, cream, yellow, pink, salmon, red

FOLIAGE
Eucalyptus  (*Eucalyptus*)

brown floss
French Knot

brown floss
Stem Stitch

dk yellow-green 4mm
Side Ribbon Stitch

Note: Although there are many varieties of *Eucalyptus* trees and shrubs, only the Silver Dollar Gum is considered here because it is frequently used in fresh and dried flower arrangements and is a good filler plant. Use floss to Stem-Stitch stems.
Leaves: Work two Side Ribbon Stitches (4 or 7mm) with bases and tips touching, alternating along branch. Use floss to work French Knots for fruiting capsules.

Boston Fern (*Nephrolepis*)

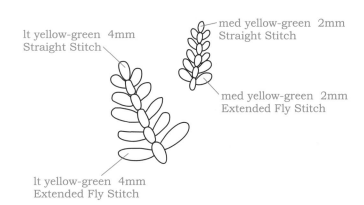

lt yellow-green 4mm
Straight Stitch

med yellow-green 2mm
Straight Stitch

med yellow-green 2mm
Extended Fly Stitch

lt yellow-green 4mm
Extended Fly Stitch

Work a Straight Stitch for the leaf tip followed by increasingly larger Extended Fly Stitches (2 or 4mm).

Maidenhair Fern (*Adiantum*)

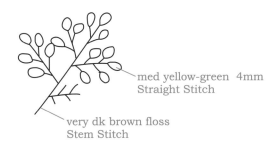

med yellow-green 4mm
Straight Stitch

very dk brown floss
Stem Stitch

Use floss to Stem-Stitch stems. Work short Straight Stitches for leaves.

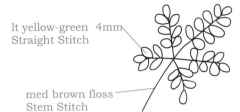
Use floss to Stem-Stitch stems. Work increasingly
larger Straight Stitches (2 or 4mm) along a
branched stem.

lt yellow-green 4mm
Straight Stitch

med brown floss
Stem Stitch

(Triticum) 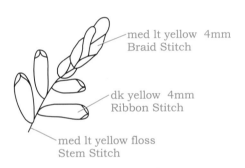 *Wheat*

Stalk: Use floss to Stem-Stitch stem. Work a
column of Braid Stitches downward to reach top of
stem.
Leaves: Work Ribbon Stitches alternating along
stem.
Flower head color: yellow, gold, brown; immature
wheat is green.

med lt yellow 4mm
Braid Stitch

dk yellow 4mm
Ribbon Stitch

med lt yellow floss
Stem Stitch

GARDEN CRITTERS

Ant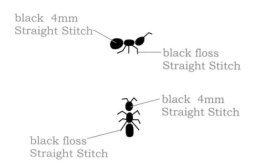

black 4mm
Straight Stitch

black floss
Straight Stitch

black 4mm
Straight Stitch

black floss
Straight Stitch

Work three Straight Stitches (2 or 4mm) in a row. Make the first stitch short and rounded for the head. Make the second stitch the same length as the first, but pull it more tightly to form the narrow body. Make the third stitch larger and more loosely than the first two stitches.

Use a single strand of floss to work Straight Stitches for the antenna(e) and legs (three per side).

Bee

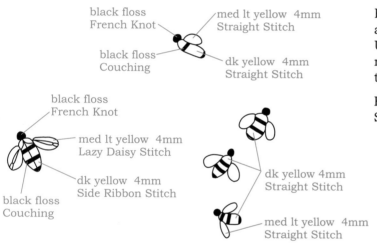

black floss
French Knot

med lt yellow 4mm
Straight Stitch

black floss
Couching

dk yellow 4mm
Straight Stitch

black floss
French Knot

med lt yellow 4mm
Lazy Daisy Stitch

dk yellow 4mm
Side Ribbon Stitch

black floss
Couching

dk yellow 4mm
Straight Stitch

med lt yellow 4mm
Straight Stitch

For body, work two Side Ribbon Stitches with tips and bases touching or a Straight Stitch (2 or 4mm). Use three to six strands of floss to Couch across ribbon body for stripes, and work a French Knot for the head.

For wings, work Lazy Daisy Stitches or a Straight Stitch (2 or 4mm) in white, cream, or lt yellow.

Butterfly

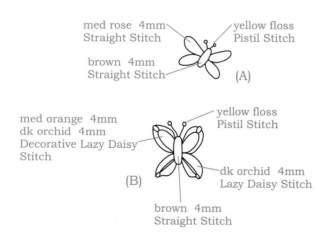

med rose 4mm
Straight Stitch

yellow floss
Pistil Stitch

brown 4mm
Straight Stitch

(A)

med orange 4mm
dk orchid 4mm
Decorative Lazy Daisy
Stitch

yellow floss
Pistil Stitch

(B)

dk orchid 4mm
Lazy Daisy Stitch

brown 4mm
Straight Stitch

For a small butterfly (A), work Straight Stitch (2, 4 or 7mm) for body and wings. Use floss to work Pistil Stitches for the antennae.

For a large butterfly (B), work Straight Stitch for the body. Work Decorative Lazy Daisy Stitch for the upper pair of wings and Lazy Daisy Stitch for the lower pair; the center stitch on the Decorative Lazy Daisy should be of a color to match the lower wings. Use floss to work Pistil Stitches for the antennae.

Note: We show two methods for making dragon-flies.
Method A—Work a very short Straight Stitch for the upper body and a long Straight Stitch for the lower body. Work Ribbon Stitches for wings, beginning each stitch by working through the body Straight Stitch close to each edge. Use six strands of floss to make French Knots for bulbous eyes.
Method B—Work a short Straight Stitch for upper body. Use six strands of floss to work a Straight Stitch for lower body. Work Straight Stitches for wings. Use six strands of floss to make French Knots for bulbous eyes.

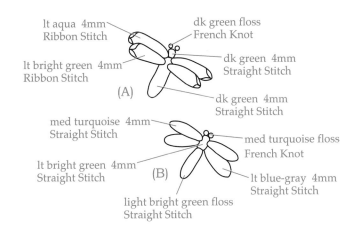

Work short, tightly pulled Backstitches for length of worm. Use floss to work Straight Stitches across worm between sections and a French Knot for eye.

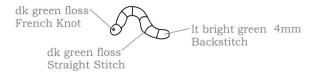

Work Straight Stitch or Side Ribbon Stitch for the body: two stitches for a full view and one stitch for a side view. Using floss, work French Knots for head and body spots, Pistil Stitches for antennae, and Straight Stitch for the separation between wings.

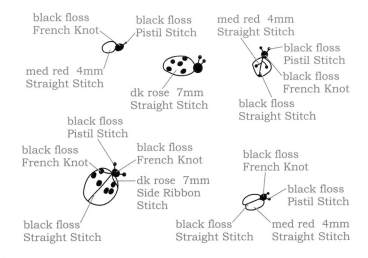

Work one short and one long Straight Stitch for the body. Begin at the center of the shell and work Whipped Running Stitch in a clockwise circle to desired size. Use floss to work Pistil Stitches for antennae.

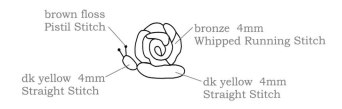

Note: We show four methods for making bows.

Method A—Pin or hold ribbon (4 or 7mm) in desired bow and streamer shape. Use floss to tack down center and decorate ribbon with French Knots.

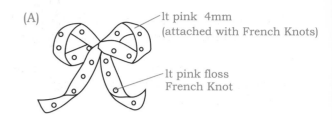

(A)

lt pink 4mm
(attached with French Knots)

lt pink floss
French Knot

Method B—Work two Loop Stitches on each side of a central point. Work a Padded Straight Stitch to cover center.

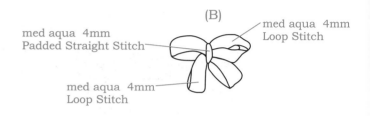

(B)

med aqua 4mm
Loop Stitch

med aqua 4mm
Padded Straight Stitch

med aqua 4mm
Loop Stitch

Method C—Stitch down into fabric and back up a short distance to the left. Pull through so two streamers of the same length extend from front of fabric. Tie a bow and trim ends. Use matching floss to tack bow securely.

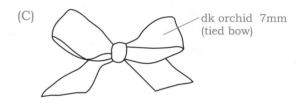

(C)

dk orchid 7mm
(tied bow)

Method D—Work Whipped Running Stitch to create a bow shape.

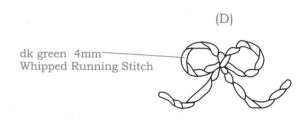

(D)

dk green 4mm
Whipped Running Stitch